*"A Child Called 'It' meets* Out of A ⸻ ⸻ *memoir of a woman's 1950s childhood in Kenya. Filled with candid humor and insights, this authentic tale captures one woman's incredible coming-of-age journey."* BookBub

140+ 4/5* US Amazon Reader Endorsements

*"A dysfunctional families true story that had me shedding real tears in some places and laughing out loud in other places as I read. A marvellous book."*

*"Spellbinding. I didn't want to put it down."*

*"This memoir kept me up. I could not stop reading this. An almost idyllic early girlhood that becomes more and more dysfunctional. What a story!"*

*"I'm sure autobiographies can be a form of therapy but this one must have been the most painful book to write. I read it in one session. There is humor and there is humanity."*

*"I read this book almost without stopping."*

*"At one point I was almost ready to shout at the book: No, no don't do it! The whole story is a great tug on the heart strings. I couldn't put the book down and have every intention of reading it again."*

*"What an astounding story, sometimes true life experiences are better than fiction."*

*"Great, engaging, memoir. Funny and very sad at times."*

# I Wish I Could Say I Was Sorry

Susie Kelly

# I Wish I Could Say I Was Sorry

Susie Kelly

**Blackbird Digital Books**
**London**

Blackbird Digital Books
London 2013
First published by Blackbird Digital Books 2013
© Susie Kelly 2013
The moral right of the author has been asserted.
The author has changed the names of many family members
Cover design Elite Cover Artwork Factory
ISBN-13: 9780993092220

*In very loving memory of*

*Florence Elsie Kelly, 17th June 1894 – 22nd December 1981*

*Florence Rosalind Kelly, 25<sup>th</sup> October 1918 – December 1967*

# CONTENTS

Prologue
Chapter 1 – Hanworth 3
Chapter 2 – Kenya Castle 15
Chapter 3 – Nairobi 22
Chapter 4 – The Anniversary Clock 32
Chapter 5 – Gertrude's Garden 36
Chapter 6 – Clapham Junction 42
Chapter 7 – The Surrey Hills 59
Chapter 8 – Holidays 71
Chapter 9 – Homesick 75
Chapter 10 – Darned Darning 81
Chapter 11 – Homeward Bound 87
Chapter 12 – Changing Schools 91
Chapter 13 – Home Truth 95
Chapter 14 – The Day Of Eggs 98
Chapter 15 – Machakos 102
Chapter 16 – Cinderella 117
Chapter 17 – Mummy 131
Chapter 18 – A Working Woman 137
Chapter 19 – Moving Out and On 142
Chapter 20 – Mary's Hall 149
Chapter 21 – Riverside 152
Chapter 22 – A Rock and a Hard Place 157
Chapter 23 – La Suocera 161
Chapter 24 – Quella la! 169
Chapter 25 – The Blessing 175
Chapter 26 – Motherhood 180
Chapter 27 – Hertfordshire 187
Chapter 28 – Smoked Salmon and Lambrusco 193

Chapter 29 – Endgame 199
Chapter 30 – Final Curtain 207
Epilogue – 213
Photographs – 217
Acknowledgements – 234

# Prologue

Not long ago I was browsing around Emmaüs in Poitiers. For anybody who doesn't know about the Emmaüs movement, it's a charity that was started by a French hero, Henri Marie Joseph Grouès, more commonly known as Abbé Pierre, who fought ferociously for the rights of the poor and underprivileged. People donate all kinds of things to the movement, from clothes and furnishings to vehicles and valuables. Nothing is wasted. Even nails and screws are carefully collected, sorted and put where they can be found. The shops are a treasure trove for anybody looking for discontinued parts for ancient machines, or collectors and dealers seeking items to sell on for profit.

It's like a giant jumble sale. For a few cents you can buy interesting, pretty items, and in buying them help individuals and families in need. I go there for crockery and glassware because I like unusual things and unmatched table settings.

On my last visit I wandered down to the far end where they sell valuable items that are kept locked up in glass cases. It was the first time I'd ever looked at that part. Next to that are shelves with large ornaments on them, and as I ran my eyes over them, I noticed a collection of clocks. Anniversary clocks. My heart lurched, the room seemed to swim, and I had to get out of there. I put down the plates I had intended to buy and rushed down the stairs, outside into the rain.

# Chapter One

# Hanworth

*Can a child be born strange?* Or does it come from some early forgotten experience? My parents and my maternal grandmother, Nan, were loving and caring; we ate well (especially considering that this was just after the end of WWII and many foods were still rationed). Our grey house was comfortable and warm, I had plenty of toys and rag books that Mummy and Nan read to me. I don't think I lacked for anything. *So why would I steal?*

At the age of five I was a thief. I had a mania for stealing paper. When I could get to school before anybody else, I went around the classroom lifting the lids of the other children's desks and digging into their exercise books with their lined and squared pages. Then, holding my breath with concentration and excitement, quickly, carefully, I would pull out several pages from the centre of each book, bending back any give-away staples that had worked loose. A new day had made a most satisfying start. Why, or what I did with the reams of paper I must have accumulated, I haven't the faintest idea. In our class only my exercise books glowed with plump good health, while my classmates' books were gaunt and skeletal, but the strange thing was that nobody ever seemed to notice. Nothing was mentioned, neither by the victims, nor by the teachers. Each day's anticipation of being named and shamed meant that I was very frightened, but at the same time strangely excited.

Encouraged by my success I began to supplement my paper reserve with money, which had a more practical benefit. Most of the other children in my class brought a 1d. (one penny piece) to school for break-time (this was the 1950s, when there were 12 pennies in a shilling). One penny might not sound much today, but it was sufficient then to buy a fine break-time treat – a choice of a pink or white sugar mouse with a little string tail, Ovaltine or Horlicks tablets folded into a small cone made from paper from used arithmetic exercise books, a packet of lemonade powder eaten from a licked finger, or a small thin chocolate bar. I don't know whether I didn't have my own penny because my parents didn't know about it, or couldn't afford it. In any event it didn't matter because as we stood beside our desks for morning prayers, our hands devoutly folded and eyes piously squeezed shut, I reached out and felt for the penny pieces nearest to me, put on the corner of their desks by their unsuspecting owners. With a nimble movement my hand found the coins and transferred them into the pocket of my gymslip. On a bumper day I managed to scoop two coins, careful not to let them clink together as they changed ownership. Astonishingly, none of my classmates ever mentioned the loss of their pennies, just as they didn't appear to notice that their exercise books were showing signs of anorexia. If I'd had a penny to lose you can be pretty sure I would have raised quite a storm if it had disappeared. So each day some unfortunate child, or on a good day, two children, didn't get a sugar mouse or similar treat. The Lord helps those who help themselves, and he certainly provided very nicely for me.

Apart from paper and pennies I began to find small, interesting items in other children's desks. Like a jackdaw I pecked them up. My satchel was a repository of things that did not belong to me – hair grips, pencils, tiny ornaments. It was the mother-of-pearl rosary beads and Bible that led to my downfall. On an early-morning raid, I was enthralled to find these pretty items in another child's desk. I slipped them into my satchel, so thrilled with this exceptional haul that I didn't even bother about harvesting any paper.

That evening there was a knock at our front door, a rare event, and my mother came and said there was someone to see me. It was the previous owner of my swag, with her parents.

*It's only now, as I write this, that I think: How had they known where to come? How had they known it was me? It's most unlikely that they would have gone to the house of each child in the class. They wouldn't have had a car, in those days almost nobody did, so they would have either had to walk or travel by bus. I'm sure, now, that they had somehow known who the thief was and come straight to our house. Is it possible that my clandestine stealing sessions were observed, not as secret as I thought? Was I watched as I pilfered? Did the watcher know about the pennies and the paper?*

"Susan," asked my mother, "did you bring home some things belonging to Angela?" The dispossessed little girl gazed at me, wide-eyed and open-mouthed.

"Yes," I said. I was a thief, not a liar.

"Then will you go and get them, and give them back like a good girl?"

Off I trotted and with a slight reluctance returned the pretty things to their owner. Then everybody made a great fuss of me. Angela's mother invited me to tea at their house, where she gave me a packet of waxed crayons and a new Bible. I never wanted to steal anything again.

Post-war London, where I was born, was a landscape in every shade of grey. Our semi-detached house was grey, in a grey road in a grey place called Hanworth in the now administratively-defunct county of Middlesex, south-west London.

At that time, we were a respectable middle-class family, like hundreds of thousands of similar families. My mild and gentle father worked for Kodak, and Mummy was a housewife and mother. We were the only family in the street who owned a motor vehicle – a motorcycle and sidecar my father used for travelling to and from work, and for pleasure rides. Mummy rode on the pillion with her arms around my father and I sat in the little pod with its slightly hazy plastic windows. We had a black cat called Clem, named after Clement Attlee, the British Prime Minister. Clem's favourite spot was curled up asleep in my father's old leather attaché case in the garden.

On Sunday mornings my father liked to walk, and if I went with him I had to jog smartly to keep up with his long stride. Those walks took us to nearby Teddington Lock on the river Thames, and Royal Bushy Park where we played cricket, my father bowling slow balls and me trying to whack them back with a child's cricket bat. The highlight of our visits to the park was a ride on Bonny Bright Eyes, the playground rocking horse that seated several passengers.

At weekends, Mummy's mother, Nan, came to visit with her corgi, Taffy. During the war she, like so many others had 'dug for victory' and it was something she had enjoyed and continued. She spent Saturdays weeding, hoeing, sowing, planting, staking and harvesting boxes of beautiful vegetables and fruit. Short, dignified and plump, she was beautifully spoken and always impeccably dressed. Her passion was music. Both her paternal grandparents were opera singers; her father was a chorister at Westminster Abbey and her uncle a chorister at St Paul's Cathedral. She had trained to be an opera singer and sung in the chorus of many operas with the great names of the time. Later, when her voice began to let her down she became a secretary, and worked for one of the senior directors of the General Electric Company. During the First World War she had married an American serviceman and emigrated to the United States. It was an unhappy marriage and after two years she returned to England with her little daughter – my mother. Although she never mentioned it, the stigma and difficulties of being a divorcée and single mother in the 1920s must have been considerable.

She was the quintessentially doting grandmother who would do and give me anything I asked for. For a while I had an obsession with posting presents to myself. Nan would find small things like her powder compact, a tiny scent bottle or a writing pad, and together we carefully wrapped them in brown paper, tied them with string and addressed to me. Then we walked hand-in-hand to the Post Office to buy stamps and drop the packet into the letter box. When it was delivered the following day I was beside myself with excitement. A week or so later it was recycled and re-posted, and no matter how many times I sent myself the same thing, the delight of receiving it never diminished.

Our next door neighbour was a tall, thin man with a long black beard, always dressed in black and always wearing a large black hat. Whenever our paths crossed he smiled and said "Hello". My father hurried me past, telling me not to speak to him because he was a Jew. I asked once what a Jew was as he looked much like any other person, but my father simply said they weren't like us. I tried pressing the question, in what way weren't they like us, but there didn't seem to be a proper explanation. I spent the next twenty years wondering exactly what it was about Jews that made them 'not like us'. It's strange that such a quiet and easy-going man as my father should have been a bigot. He also hated Germans which was more understandable, as he'd served in the British army for the duration of WWII and his uncle had been killed at Dunkirk.

Directly opposite our house lived Mummy's friend Auntie Kitty. Tall and thin with a chuckly voice, wiry black hair and a prominent wart on her chin, Auntie Kitty became a celebrity in our street when she bought a television in 1953 so that she and we could watch the Coronation. I recall that the sound was very clear – the harsh, unfaltering voice of our new Queen as she made her first public address, although the black and white picture flickered on and off and the small screen seemed to be enveloped in a snow storm. It was a freezing day and a long afternoon, punctuated by servings of Auntie Kitty's speciality. Soaked in a mixture of egg and milk, cooked in lard and saturated with sugar, her fried jam sandwiches were ambrosial. When Auntie Kitty's big chin wart began sprouting hairs, Mummy persuaded her to do something about it, and so we went by bus with her one day to hospital to have it removed. All the way home we laughed at her delight in not having the thing on her chin any more. Wherever Mummy was, there was always laughter.

Once a year we went on holiday with Nan to Boscombe, east of Bournemouth on England's south coast. After breakfast at the guesthouse on the Lansdowne Road, we marched down the long zigzag path to the sandy beach with its fascinating pools of slimy, podded weed and furtive creatures scuttling and darting beneath rocks. My ruched red swimming costume held water, so as I emerged from the sea it drooped around my knees as the water drained away.

Looking back, I recall the weather was always perfect, never a cloud or drop of rain to spoil the blue of the sky and the kiss of the sun. Boscombe meant being with my parents and Nan all day, every day, ice cream, pony rides, mini-golf, building sandcastles and then watching the incoming tide melt them away. At the end of the day the haul back up the long zigzag path was hard work for small, tired legs.

Those memories of the early years of my life are of security and love. As my father was at work I saw less of him than Mummy, and he was not as demonstrative as her, but I adored him.

I have pin clear mental photos of our life in Hanworth.

On the kitchen table sit rows of fragrant small sponge cakes in fluted wax paper cases. When they are cool, Mummy slices off the tops and cuts them in half. She spreads butter cream over the base and sticks the two pieces on top, like wings. She calls them 'Butterfly cakes', and always leaves a generous amount of delicious raw cake mixture in the mixing bowl for me to eat with a wooden spoon. Even today when I make a cake and take a spoonful of the raw mixture and close my eyes, I see and smell the butterfly cakes on our kitchen table.

While I sit on the draining board with my feet in the kitchen sink, Mummy works her way down from my face to my feet with a flannel dipped in the warm, soapy water. When she washes my hair she gives me a flannel to press against my eyes to stop the shampoo stinging them. We run our fingers through my wet hair. If it squeaks then we know it's clean. Then she wraps me in a towel and pats me dry, feeds me into my pyjamas and warm blue dressing gown with the ladybird buttons.

The dressing gown has a cord of twisted blue and silver, with tassels on the end. Alone in the living room in front of the coal fire covered by a wire safety guard, I swing the dressing gown's tasselled cord into the flames so that it singes with a satisfying sizzly noise and an interesting smell. Mummy sniffs when she comes into the room, and looks in puzzlement at the carpet in front of the fire for signs of smouldering.

The fire can be a bit of a sod to start. My father holds sheets of newspaper across the sullen chimney to encourage the draught. Putrid smoke billows, then a small flame grows, singeing the paper yellow. Half an hour later the coals glow orange as we sit listening to the radio. Clem gets as close as he can to the fire. Mummy knits or smocks clothes for me and my father puffs on his pipe.

All our walls are painted the same dull cream colour, so my father decorates the living room with a bucket of distemper. It's a thick green stuff the colour of baby's diarrhoea, and he blobs it onto the wall with a roller. It looks horrible.

At weekends Nan is in the garden with Taffy, rain or shine, always planting or picking. I don't remember Mummy doing anything in the garden apart from rescuing birds from Clem. She stows them tenderly into a cardboard shoe box and puts them in the airing cupboard to recover. Usually they regain their senses and equilibrium after a couple of hours, and fly away to safety. Or straight back into Clem. Daddy doesn't garden, either, but he likes pansies because they have happy little faces.

Nan eats Energen Rolls because she is trying to lose weight. They are crispy on the outside and crispy within, but not very satisfying. I prefer Taffy's charcoal dog biscuits.

Once we go to visit Daddy's parents. There is a long, gloomy, dark green corridor and two and a half flights of stairs. At the top is a bedroom where a skeletal yellow-skinned woman lies in bed coughing.

Mummy comes home from the Ideal Homes Exhibition, merry, footsore and laden with carrier bags stuffed with miniature pots of jam.

She takes me to Bentalls in Kingston to have my hair cut, and then we have tea and toasted teacakes oozing with butter. We bring home one of their cakes shaped like a giant mushroom and made from marzipan and lashings of coffee cream.

Every Friday evening she coos with delight over a box of powdery Turkish delight, Payne's Poppets or Buttered Brazil Nuts, her weekly treat from Daddy.

She is always happy, smiling and beautiful, with short curly dark hair, golden hazel eyes and a carefully-pencilled black beauty spot to the side of her mouth.

In the summer she ties ribbons in my silver blonde hair, and sews pretty smocked dresses. During the winter months I wear a pair of rust-coloured Harris tweed leggings, and a liberty bodice beneath a knitted jumper. The leggings are thick hairy trousers with a broad elastic band that passes underneath my shoes to hold the trousers down over my ankles. Wearing them can best be likened to having both legs scrubbed with medium grade steel wool: they have an abrasive quality that makes each step torture. Mummy takes great pride in dressing me in style, and these horrid trousers must be the *dernier cri*. She can't have the least idea of what torment it is to wear them. The liberty bodice is a less painful, more private garment, a short, white fleecy sleeveless thing with rubber buttons and little rubbery suspenders to hold up the thick brown wrinkly stockings that we wear to school; it fits under a chunky woolly vest that lies beneath various other layers of clothing culminating in a hand-knitted jumper all designed to keep the penetrating damp of English winters at bay. My hair is tucked beneath a bright red knitted pixie bonnet, tight-fitting like a snood and reaching to a nipple on the crown of my head. The rust-coloured leggings and the red pixie hat add quite a splash of colour to the generally grey environment.

On my sideboard today is a sepia photograph of a handsome blonde five-year-old boy. He's wearing a one-piece woollen bathing costume with straps over the shoulders, sitting on a rock on a beach, smiling into the sun. This is my brother Ian, born in October of 1940, the height of the Blitz on London.

I suppose it was because Mummy would have been working during the war that he was sent to live with an elderly couple in Devon. All I know is that in February 1945, Ian's temporary foster parents wrote to tell Mummy that he was ill, with a seemingly permanent cold. She went to Devon, where the doctor told her that Ian had meningitis. There was no treatment, no cure and no hope. It was only a matter of time. He died with Mummy sitting by his bed and his father in North Africa. I cannot begin to imagine how they were affected by this loss, how my father felt when he learned the news, so far away, and how my mother coped with the loss of her child as well as the absence of and worry about her husband.

Probably it was for this sad reason that my birthday and Christmas presents were always things like a bus conductor's costume, complete with a punching machine and tickets, or a Meccano set in the form of a crane with a little handle to wind it up and down to pick up matchboxes. My father made small contraptions from a cotton reel, a rubber band and a length of candle. When the rubber band had been twisted sufficiently the cotton reel jerked across the floor in a purposeful way like a little tank. I was never given the things I really wanted, and asked for repeatedly: a glass eye, a hearing aid, and a set of false teeth. I still don't have any of them.

Each year, Kodak held a party at their offices in Kingsway, London for the children of their staff. Whether all the children found it as much of an ordeal as I did, I don't know. But none of us knew each other and I seem to remember that I couldn't wait to go home, with my slice of cake, balloon and gift-wrapped present.

There were only two things that darkened my days and nights. The monster that lived upstairs in the toilet bowl, skulking with evil intentions until the toilet was flushed, when it would spring out and rake at people's bottoms with hooked claws and spiky teeth. From terror of these awful assaults I developed a technique of opening the door wide, reaching in and yanking on the chain and leaping down the adjacent staircase before the monster could get me, crashing to the bottom of the stairs with my knickers around my ankles and alarming Mummy.

And there was Mr Beeblesticks, who lived in the big wardrobe in my bedroom (where I hid from Mummy and the knife – I'll come to that later). Mr Beeblesticks was a friend by day, but at night, once the bedroom light was turned out he became a gun-wielding murderer. So that his bullets would miss, I lay in my bed rocking madly from side to side. The rocking habit lasted until I got married, I just couldn't get to sleep unless I kept madly rolling backwards and forwards.

I didn't mention either of these horrors to my parents, because I didn't want to worry them.

*Where did these strange ideas originate, these evil people who wanted to kill me?* I was safe, secure and very well loved. The Saturday morning matinees at the cinema showed only cartoons, and the most violent programs I watched on Auntie Kitty's television were Bill and Ben the Flowerpot Men, Andy Pandy, Noddy and

11

Muffin the Mule.

Even stranger was the recurring nightmare I had for years. I was alone on an empty, sandy beach on a hot sunny day, with cliffs rising close behind me. As I watched the surf swishing gently backwards and forwards, the sea suddenly began to withdraw to the far horizon, leaving just the clean sand behind. Soon there was no sea at all, just the pristine beach. In the far distance a darkness appeared on the skyline. It began moving towards where I was standing. As it neared, it developed into a great wave, curling upwards. It rushed quickly forwards. It grew until it was the height of the cliffs behind, and I was beneath it, looking up, knowing that now the water would come crashing down and wash me away.

I'd certainly never heard of or seen a tsunami, so where did this image come from? Was it an omen, a warning of what was to come?

But these were only small blips in a very happy and normal family life filled with love and laughs and cuddles and hugs.

The convent school where I went to appropriate anything light enough to lift, not nailed down and small enough to fit in my satchel was in Sunbury-on-Thames, two bus-rides from Hanworth. Mummy walked me to the nearest bus stop, a couple of hundred yards from our house and put me on the first bus. This bus stopped at Sunbury-on-Thames where I changed to a second bus, which stopped a short distance from the school. From the bus stop I crossed a major road, although at that time there was little traffic, and then walked up a long winding rhododendron-lined drive. It's unthinkable to imagine five-year-old children undertaking such a journey alone these days, but at that time it was perfectly normal. One small girl in our class caught a train unaccompanied to and from school. At her invitation I went home with her one day, to the considerable consternation of her mother who had no idea she was expecting a guest. She had to take me back by train and bus to where my mother was panicking at my failure to arrive home.

In the classroom, before reading or writing, or sums or drawing we learned the Ten Commandments. We learned them by heart, by constant chanted repetition: Thou shalt not this, thou shalt not that. You mustn't do idolatry or adultery and you mustn't steal (I think that was No. 7). If you did any of these things then you could not go to Heaven. Instead you would burn in Purgatory and have to suffer very much indeed forever and ever; but even this fearsome prospect did not deter or frighten me from stealing paper and money, despite the great black sin blotches I knew were printed all over my wicked little soul, which would be a dead giveaway on the Day of Judgement.

We were not a religious family. I think we called ourselves Church of England, but as far as I remember the family only went to church to deliver me to Sunday school. Like my weekly dancing and elocution lessons, a convent education would, my parents believed, make me into a little lady.

The only time I ever remember Mummy being angry was when I was eating. I was a slow eater and had difficulty swallowing. It wasn't that I was fussy. I'd eat anything except angelica, with which Mummy decorated the trifle, but I could chew soup or ice cream for hours on end, churning it around and around in my mouth like cement swishing in a mixer, until Mummy screamed: "For God's sake, *swallow* it!" But the harder I tried, the less I could swallow, so I chewed and swished faster and faster. One day when I was struggling with a mouthful of tomato soup, she picked up a knife and frightened me so much I ran upstairs and shut myself in the wardrobe where Mr Beeblesticks lived.

When I ventured out, Mummy was sitting sobbing on my bed, and I don't know which of us was the more traumatised.

After that I ate my meals with our friends the Mason family who lived on the opposite side of the fence at the bottom of our garden. Daddy removed a plank from the fence so that I didn't have to go around by the road. The Masons had a little boy called Charles, who was quite happy for me to sit churning in their dining room while he watched and waited patiently for the final gulp that released us to play. He must have been quite a precocious little boy, because the game we played most was 'r' for rudies, which mainly consisted of watching each other urinate into a small bowl in his bedroom. I think I probably got more out of this than he did. The casual way he asked in front of his parents if I wanted to go and play 'r' used to make me hot and crimson with embarrassment. I was certain that his mother and father were perfectly aware of our urinary adventures.

One morning, left to our own devices, Charles and I raided my house of anything small enough to lift, and set it all outside to sell. In those days there was almost no motor traffic about. Milk and coal were still delivered by horse-drawn carts, policemen patrolled on foot and people went to work by public transport, so we could safely spread out our wares across the street without worrying. Whose idea this had been or why, I'm not sure, but possibly we'd run out of urine. Nan arrived just in time to save Mummy's twelve treasured Apostle spoons going off with a stranger for one penny.

# Chapter Two
# Kenya Castle

In 1954, I turned eight. In the diarrhoea-coloured front room a dozen of my school friends were enjoying jam tarts, butterfly cakes, lemon curd sandwiches with the crusts removed, jelly in waxed paper bowls and a pink blancmange rabbit. We were having a party to celebrate not only my birthday, but also some very exciting news. Mummy clapped her hands, and two rows of little faces gawped at her as she put a finger to her lips, signalling silence. Soon, she said, our family would be leaving England and going to live in Africa. We all clapped enthusiastically and shouted "Hurray!" It was a shame that my friends wouldn't be coming with us, but on the other hand it was going to be a great adventure. Based on a Tarzan film I'd recently seen I expected our new home to be a tree house reached by swinging through the jungle on trailing foliage. I could already see myself waving to passing monkeys and riding around on elephants. I couldn't wait to get there.

In August 1954, we climbed into a taxi and left the grey house in the grey street to spend our last night in England at a hotel in central London. Driving through the streets we passed rows and blocks of buildings crumbling into chunks of brick and clouds of dust. Great iron balls swung from cranes into walls, collapsing them likes castles of cards. As the walls fell away they revealed wallpaper and pictures still hanging in rooms that would never be lived in again. It was like looking at a collection of broken dolls' houses. Nine years after the end of WWII, parts of London were still in a frightful mess.

The hotel was a palace of thick carpets, long corridors, polished banisters, sumptuous rooms and electric lights left on all the time.

Sitting in the grand dining room for our evening meals and breakfasts the following morning, I imagined that even our new Queen couldn't be living in greater splendour than we were.

Nan had come to see us off at Tilbury docks. She had already lost a grandson; now she was here to see her only child and granddaughter leaving to live more than 4,000 miles away, in a country in a state of emergency due to the Mau Mau uprising. With our departure she'd have no family left in England. It would be four years before we'd see her again, when my father's first long leave would be due and we'd all come back to England for a holiday. Or that is what we thought.

The gangway trembled as we boarded the S. S. Kenya Castle. Elegant, red-funnelled, lavender-coloured, one of the fleet of the Union Castle Steamship Company, she would take us to our new life. Noise and confusion, seamen scurrying around, luggage being hauled aboard, paper streamers in the air, a feeling of elation tinged with sadness. As the liner pulled away from the docks to the mournful blaring of the ship's horn, Mummy cried. We waved to the tiny figure of Nan standing on the dock far below, one hand raised in a sad farewell, growing ever smaller as the ship pulled away, until she was gone from sight.

In those days air travel was a relatively new and far more expensive method of travel, something reserved for the wealthy. But for us life aboard this opulent floating hotel was indescribably exciting. From the grey street in Hanworth and the routine of everyday life we were transported to a new world. Our cabin was luxurious, with its own bathroom. There was a swimming pool, games rooms, cinemas, libraries, shops and an ever-changing and ever more colourful scenery. The dining tables wore starched white linen cloths, and the menus changed daily. Fourteen years of food rationing in Britain had only ended in July; breakfast at home had been toast and jam or marmalade. Now we could choose from a variety of cereals, stewed and fresh fruits that became increasingly exotic as the ship ploughed southwards; eggs cooked to order, kidneys, kippers, bacon, sausages, kedgeree, toast and butter and a choice of jams. We were spoiled for choice. At mid-morning each

16

day, white-uniformed stewards walked the decks where passengers sat on chairs or loungers with blankets over their knees, serving cups of hot Bovril. As we advanced southwards, Bovril gave way to strawberry and vanilla ice creams in little cartons eaten with wooden spatulas. At home they had been an occasional summer treat, but now were in abundance. There was a daily quota of these ice creams, and any surplus was tossed overboard, to bob and swirl in the foaming wake of the ship. I was sorry I couldn't eat more, but even ice cream took a lot of chewing.

Lunch was another feast, followed by afternoon tea served in the library. Instead of the Sandwich Spread or Shippams fish paste sandwiches that had been our staple tea in Hanworth, there were tiered trays of neat triangular sandwiches, dainty iced cakes and tea poured from silver teapots into china cups.

Children's evening meal was served early, before the adults who were expected to dress formally for dinner. I used to sit in my pyjamas on a balcony, looking down on the dining room where glasses chinked and waiters weaved between the tables with laden trays. My father, tall and very slim with fair hair and a neat matching moustache, and Mummy with her sparkling eyes and wide smile were a striking couple. To me they were indisputably the most glamorous parents on the ship, standing out amongst the crowd, dancing after dinner in each other's arms to the ship's orchestra.

Every day there were organised activities – films, games and fancy dress competitions – I won a prize as a little pink crepe-paper rosebud. Deck games for adults – quoits, clay pigeon shooting, crazy races and the daily sweepstake that involved calculating how far the ship would progress during the next twenty-four hours. Passengers enjoyed constant entertainment from morning to night, day after day. All day, every day. Mummy, Daddy and me together.

The Kenya Castle carved her way down the western coast of France, through the Bay of Biscay and along the Spanish and Portuguese coastline, stopping in Gibraltar where we laughed at the antics of the apes. In the Mediterranean heat, Mummy and I flagged and came up in itchy bumps. From his wartime service in North Africa and Italy, Daddy was less affected, although his fair complexion resembled a boiled prawn. In Port Said and Port Sudan, we sat at rickety tables in dirty places, drinking hot lemonade and batting at clouds of flies and bluebottles that swarmed around our faces, sipped from the spill on the tables and crawled into our sticky glasses.

I'll never forget sailing through the Suez Canal. Silhouettes of camels, donkeys, men and children glided past on the palmy sandbanks as the sun folded itself from a brilliant red ball into a sliver that slid gracefully from sight into the blackness of the night. During the day hordes of noisy Arab children besieged the ship, clambering up rope ladders from little boats, winching up to the decks leather pouffes and whips, camel stools, brassware, all manner of interesting and exciting things, and screaming prices that halved, halved and halved again until a deal was struck. The magic gully-gully man in his long white robe sat cross-legged on the deck and produced from thin air, our pockets or the backs of our necks tiny yellow chicks until the deck was overrun with little balls of yellow fuzz. The heat was stifling, and my nose bled copiously. Where the Suez Canal issued into the Red Sea, we stopped in the unspeakable heat of Aden for cheap duty-free shopping.

The Red Sea bled into the Indian Ocean as we followed the African coastline. Crossing the Equator poor King Neptune, in keeping with tradition had to be dunked into the swimming pool, and I seem to remember that he had a bucket of eggs thrown over him too for our entertainment.

When we hove into Kilindini docks in Mombasa, my first feeling was one of tremendous disappointment. There were tarmac roads, modern buildings, motor vehicles and not a single tree house, jungle or elephant in sight. But the disappointment was fleeting, erased by the noise of cranes unloading cargo, the rattling of unleashed chains, ships' horns moaning, vehicles hooting. Laughing barefoot Africans dressed in only khaki shorts glistened black beneath the sun, heaving loads and pushing top-heavy wobbly wooden carts. The smell was of salt water and spices, hot tar, hot leather luggage and sweat. It was a scene completely alien to anything I could have imagined, and overwhelmingly seductive.

Once our luggage was unloaded and processed in the corrugated iron shed that was the Customs Office, we moved on to the final stage of our safari, the train journey from Mombasa to Nairobi, on what was known as the Lunatic Line. I am really very grateful to Linda Watanabe McFerrin[1] for giving permission to quote from her article, first published in the San Francisco Examiner/Chronicle Sunday Travel Section.

*"I sat back on my narrow bunk on the Kenya Railways train that runs nightly from Nairobi to Mombasa, pulled up the window shade and surveyed the exterior landscape. Outside the railcar, the dark continent was truly dark. I saw giraffe, elephants, wildebeest, zebra – herds of fantastic ebony creatures on the move. But, in truth, they were only baobab trees, kapoks, thorn trees, bush – denizens of the vegetable kingdom transformed, by starlight and my imagination, into animals. By day, the high plains around Nairobi would, in fact, be grazed by these creatures, but for now – moving in comforting shadow toward slumber – this menagerie of fancy seemed most appropriate. I was, after all, aboard the Lunatic Express, a line that, to conventional minds, had always been a bit far-fetched.*

*"It was an eccentric enterprise and therefore perfectly suited to the British temperament of the late 19th Century. Nevertheless, when the Imperial British East Africa Company proposed its scheme to lay track from the East African coast into the unsettled interior, the critics stood up and raised voices. Media dubbed the proposed railway a 'lunatic line'. According to the plan, the Central African Railway, starting at Mombasa, would move through 657 miles of African bush past a little-known Masai watering hole, at the time called enkare nyarobe or 'sweet water', over the Great Rift Valley, across the equatorial highlands and down to the shores of Lake Victoria where steamships could continue the route through Uganda.*

*"It would, supporters conjectured, put an end to the slave trade which originated, in part, in Uganda and to which the British were opposed; and it would provide a route via Lake Victoria and the Nile through British East Africa that would link the ports of the Indian Ocean to the Mediterranean Sea. Of course, at the time, there was*

*no one to service along the way, but strategically, it seemed like a very sound move. They could build it at a cost of £3,685,400.*

*"They were energetic. They were optimistic. They were wrong.*

*"First, they'd have to build a new port to accommodate the supply ships. Termites would devour the wooden risers as fast as they laid them; lions would devour the workers; dysentery, tsetse flies, hostile tribes and malaria would pick off the survivors, and torrential rains would wash away what the termites had missed. It would end up costing almost twice the estimate. It would take nearly a decade to complete. At the end of the first year, they would have progressed a pitiful twenty-four miles inland.*

*"It was a heroic endeavour, and in spite of the obstacles, it was an insanely brilliant success. It made white settlement of the East African highlands possible. When completed, it shortened the journey from Mombasa to Nairobi from six weeks to twenty-four hours. But the name, 'Lunatic Express', stuck and rightly so."*

It was late afternoon when our train pulled out of Mombasa's frenzied railway station. For a short time we could watch the passing landscape of banana trees and coconut palms like vast umbrellas, thatched mud huts and, to my 8-year-old eyes, embarrassingly bare-breasted black ladies. Their naked little pot-bellied children, with teeth startlingly white against their brown skin, sat in the dust, smiling and waving enthusiastically as the train passed.

Night falls abruptly and early in Africa, and soon there was nothing to see except blackness. A steward came and converted our seats into bunk beds, made up with thick, cool white linen sheets and heavy, dark green scratchy blankets. It is a 300-mile journey to Nairobi, uphill all the way from sea level to 5,500 feet and the train struggled along the tracks, at times hardly above walking pace. We ate in the dining car at tables laid with starched white cloths and lit by small table lamps. Our meals were served by soft-voiced black men, barefoot, wearing dazzling white gloves and starched khanzu – ankle-length garments like nightshirts – and black-tasselled red fezzes on their heads. The train jolted gently through the night as it ground its way through the vast wild African countryside.

20

The next morning we raised the blinds for our first view of the dusty, flat Athi plains, 40 miles south of Nairobi. The brown landscape was dotted with thorn trees and teemed with animals – giraffe, zebras, wildebeest, warthogs, hyenas, Thompson and Grant gazelles, in their hundreds and in their thousands.

As wondrous a sight as this was, I was still concerned because there were still no signs of any tree houses, and not even the shadow of an elephant.

# Chapter Three

# Nairobi

Nairobi railway station was a cauldron of excitement, colour, stenches and commotion. Velvety, rumbling African voices and gentle laughter, urgent shouts, the occasional roar of a donkey; impatient hooting vehicles; ghastly odours of rotting vegetables enhanced by the heat of the sun already high by early morning; gleaming black skin, huge white smiles, eager hands loading luggage onto handcarts. We stood in a small family huddle amidst this new world, and despite my disappointment that it was not a liana-festooned jungle populated by wild animals and tree-houses, I was enchanted by the Technicolor magic of this foreign land.

One of my father's new colleagues arrived at the station to take us to what would be our temporary accommodation until our furniture arrived from England. He drove us to Plums Hotel up what was then known as Princess Elizabeth Highway. The wide multi-carriageway was lined with crimson Nandi flame and blue Jacaranda trees, punctuated by roundabouts ablaze with bougainvillea in all its flamboyant colours – purple, crimson, scarlet, pale orange, Persil white. Everywhere there was colour and open space and blue skies and the caress of the sun.

At the hotel we stayed in a 'banda', a self-contained cottage set amongst lush sprinkled lawns. Creamy frangipani blossoms, with their velvety orange hearts perfumed the air. Grey lizards flittered through piles of stones and up the walls, disappearing when I tried to catch them, and leaving behind their wriggling tails as a defiant souvenir. Long-tailed mousebirds bathed in the dust; bright yellow weaver birds built their intricate nest colonies and iridescent glossy

22

starlings ravaged the loquat trees. In the hotel dining room were long menus to choose from, of both familiar and completely strange dishes, particularly the fresh fruit – pineapples, bananas, sticky mangoes, sickly sweet papaya, tangy passion fruit and creamy avocado pears. Until then the most foreign fruit I'd tasted was the tangerine tucked in the toe of my Christmas stocking next to the handful of nuts and small net bag of chocolate coins.

Each night, one of the hotel staff came to the banda with a giant flit gun, and enthusiastically pumped every corner and crevice with a stinking and choking substance designed to kill mosquitoes. It probably did us more harm than them. White mosquito nets hung from the ceiling and had to be tucked in all around the edge of our beds, but there always seemed to be small holes somewhere that allowed the enterprising, resilient mosquitoes to find their way through and bite us, leaving pink itchy lumps. If you gouged a cross in the bites by digging a fingernail really hard into them it stopped the itching, until the pain from the fingernail subsided.

When our furniture arrived we moved into a spacious bungalow on the Lower Kabete Road in the area called Westlands, a residential suburb some five miles from the centre of Nairobi town. Adjacent to the bungalow was a small guesthouse where the then Governor of Kenya, Sir Evelyn Baring's secretary lived. The properties belonged to one of the most charismatic characters ever to leave his footprints on the continent of Africa, Colonel Ewart Grogan, swashbuckling pioneer and legendary hunter. He was outspoken and controversial in his views on the British administration of Kenya, owned half a million acres of land, and was the first man to walk from Cape Town to Cairo, to prove to his future father-in-law that he was of suitable matrimonial fibre.

He would have been in his 80s, a tall, upright gentleman, white-haired and white-bearded – he reminded me of pictures I'd seen of Buffalo Bill – when he arrived unannounced by taxi at our house one day. He had just remembered leaving £10,000 (a phenomenal amount today, let alone then) in notes on top of a wardrobe in one of our bedrooms. As the wardrobes were built-in and reached right to the ceiling, there was no 'on top' to them. He was very confused and anxious, and couldn't understand where the wardrobe's top had gone. He insisted on climbing on a chair to feel that it wasn't there for himself. My father drove him to the railway station to put him on a train back to Mombasa, near where he lived. Leaving me standing on the platform, my father helped him aboard, but it took so long to settle the Colonel into his carriage that the train started pulling slowly away, leaving me howling with fright at the sight of my disappearing parent, who daringly leapt from the train just before he ran out of platform.

Apart from being our landlord, the Colonel would have, indirectly, an enormous influence over my life. In memory of the wife he had walked so far to win, he had founded in her name a children's hospital in Nairobi, Gertrude's Garden. In less than a year, I would be lying in that hospital, catalysing the drama that would affect our family for decades.

The driveway to our house was lined on both sides with sisal bushes decorated with spears of creamy bells that seemed ill at ease amongst the spiky leaves. Outside the kitchen and my bedroom were pepper trees whose small pink berries susurrated in the wind. In the spacious back garden was a large clump of tall bamboo, which is where the snakes lived. We'd only been in the house a couple of weeks when the gardener decapitated a large spitting cobra; he put its body out in the road, because, he explained, its mate would come to find it and be run over. That was exactly what happened. I thought what a horribly cruel way it was to treat the snakes that had been quite contentedly living in the bamboo causing no harm to anybody. My father explained to the puzzled gardener that in future we'd just leave the snakes to themselves. There was no need to walk around the bamboo banging it with a broom to try to chase them out to be killed.

At the same time as we moved into the bungalow, my father bought a car. That may not sound revolutionary today, but to us it was a miracle – we could go anywhere, at any time, whatever the weather, like rich people. It was a Vauxhall Velox in a beautiful shade that varied between dark blue and mauve, depending on how the light caught it, like the colour of an oil spill on water. Its leather upholstery smelt and squeaked. While owning a car in England was still something of a novelty, in Kenya it was, for Europeans, a necessity. Distances were immense, and public transport, such as it was, primitive, consisting of grossly over-laden single-decker buses that carried their passengers and their livestock at breakneck speed and often to their deaths, and local taxis that were similar but on a smaller scale.

Mummy was keen to learn to drive, and my father said he would teach her. I sat in the back while we lurched and swerved along the Princess Elizabeth Highway. Provoked by Mummy's continually futile attempts to find the right gears, my father started shouting at her, and she slammed the car to a squealing halt.

"*Will* you stop yelling at me!" she yelled at him. "Next time, I'll drive this thing into the nearest lamp post."

Off we rocked again, until a new grating of gears made my father bellow: "For God's sake, use the *clutch*!"

True to her promise Mummy put the accelerator to the floor and pointed us at the next lamp post. My father grabbed the wheel; the kerb knocked some of the speed off the car, which scraped its side lightly on the post and stopped in a bougainvillea hedge. I slithered from one side to the other on the slippery back seat. My parents changed places in the front, and Mummy didn't drive the car again.

We had a servant, a 'houseboy' is what they were called. He was a dignified gentleman who cooked, and cleaned the house. He slid around the parquet floors with sheepskin fleeces under his bare feet, so that as he worked his way round he polished the floor at the same time. There was also a gardener who watered and tended the flowerbeds in the crispy, fawn-coloured lawn. Beyond the lawn was about an acre of unkempt and scrubby grass.

In our family the native people were called Africans. Often we heard Europeans using words like coon, sambo, wog, nigger, black or *nugu*, the Swahili word for a monkey. I didn't like hearing these plainly derogatory words for the people who smiled and looked after us, and sang or whistled as they worked. Our house servant was a quiet man who went about his business like a black ghost, almost unseen and unheard. His name was Jotham, and he addressed my father as *Bwana[2]*, Mummy as *Memsahib[3]*, and me as *Memsahib Kidogo[4]*. He cooked, cleaned, washed and ironed, unhurriedly and efficiently, and earned about £5 a month, the normal wage. His own living quarters, consisting of two rooms and washing facilities were twenty yards from the bungalow, and were shared with the gardener. As well as their monthly salary they were supplied with beds, a charcoal stove for cooking and a monthly ration of charcoal. It was tacitly accepted that they would help themselves to sugar, tea, milk and anything else they could get away with. When they took our milk they topped up the bottles with water, leaving an increasingly blue watery liquid.

One of my father's friends showed him how to stop the servants helping themselves to spirits. If they drew a line on the bottle at the level where the spirits reached, the servant could help himself and then top up the bottle to the line. But – if you *inverted* the bottle and then drew the line at the level of the contents, the servants were completely bamboozled.

There were many funny anecdotes. I don't know how true they were, but they always raised a laugh.

One concerned three bachelors sharing a house. Their house servant gave them a shopping list every week, and there was always a bottle of sherry on the list. One day, one of the men remarked that they seemed to get through a great deal of sherry, but none of them drank it. They concluded the servant was helping himself, and decided to give him an unpleasant surprise. Taking a half empty bottle, they topped it up with urine. The following week, the bottle was empty and back on the shopping list. It was time to challenge the servant. How was it, they asked him, that none of them drank sherry, but every week the bottle was empty and they had to buy a new one. *Bwana*, he replied, I put it in the soup.

There was also a tale of a couple who went away for a weekend to stay out of town at a primitive shack. The lavatory was a shed a few yards from the house and the toilet was a box seated over a hole. The man went out during the night, with a kerosene lamp, there being no electricity on the property, and came running back yelling that he'd been bitten on his backside by a snake. On his buttocks were two superficial bite marks. But what kind of snake was it? They dared not go back in the dark to investigate. If it was a mamba, cobra or puff adder the bite could be lethal. There was only one thing to do. The wife took a sharp knife, slashed the bite marks and then sucked out and spat away as much blood as she could to remove the venom.

When daylight came the man was showing no signs of being affected by the bites, and together they went cautiously to find the snake, armed with a shovel. Pushing open the door they peered into the box. Staring back at them from the box was an indignant hen.

Jotham's bicycle was his pride and joy, and no doubt had taken him a long time to save for. My father found him one day covered in cuts and bruises, having been knocked off his machine by a car that hadn't stopped. He took Jotham to the local dispensary where his wounds were disinfected and bandaged. The next evening we watched him pushing his bicycle up the driveway. He had removed all the bandages from himself, and wrapped them around the bicycle's frame.

Daddy was a mild-natured and quietly-spoken man without an aggressive cell in his body. He was very much distressed when one morning he politely asked Jotham whether his shoes had been polished. Jotham screamed, rolled his eyes in terror, rushed to his quarters, put on the army greatcoat that he wore in all seasons, pedalled away on his bicycle and was never seen again.

There was no shortage of capable staff; almost daily at least one man seeking work would knock at the door and hand over an envelope with his references. Once it was evident that Jotham was gone for good (and why, we'd never know) we acquired a replacement. One candidate presented a much-folded letter of reference from a local English magistrate who had recently dispensed with his services. It read: 'The bearer worked for me for one year, during which time he served us very well, and himself too. If this gentleman does you as well as he has done us, you will be well done'. The poor man was inordinately proud of the letter and no doubt puzzled at the reluctance of anybody to employ him.

Our arrival coincided with the beginning of the end of Kenya's colonial era. We caught the last few glimpses of the remnants of, for

27

the Europeans, a romantic age that was reaching its closing stages. In the 1950s, many shops and Government offices along the broad, tree-lined streets of Nairobi were no more than single-storey buildings raised on short wooden stilts, with wide verandas around them and red corrugated iron roofs on which the sound of rainfall was like a mad orchestra. Macho white farmers drove into town in rattling Land Rovers, wearing khaki shorts, chukka boots, floppy bush hats, and guns on their hips. They propped up the bars of favourite watering holes like the Long Bar at the Norfolk Hotel, downing pints, occasionally shooting up the town, and calling the Africans 'boys'.

A beautiful, exotic town of spacious avenues and blazing colours – twenty years later Nairobi would have become a concrete jungle of skyscrapers, just like any modern city anywhere in the world. An independent country ruled by its native peoples. Many white farmers would have moved on to Australia or Rhodesia, and the roads would be filled with African ministers and businessmen driving Mercedes.

With our car we could go wherever and whenever we fancied. Distance was no object. A fifteen-mile drive for tea at the Brackenhurst Hotel in the gentle green hills of at Limuru, or fifty miles through the Rift Valley to Naivasha for a picnic beside the lake were regular weekend outings. We learned not to stop for the groups of 'totos', African children lining the sides of the road offering bunches of rhubarb, baby rabbits and wooden carvings for sale. Once a car halted they wrenched the doors open and stuffed their wares in, screaming for a 'samuni' – a fifty cent piece, the equivalent of six pence. As fast as we shovelled rhubarb and carvings from the car, they forced them all back in. My father would toss a handful of change onto the side of the road to distract them, and we'd drive on with sufficient rhubarb to last for a month and baby rabbits we released further down the road.

I cannot recall a single occasion when my parents had been invited out for a meal when we lived in England, except for Kodak's annual staff dinner, nor anybody coming to eat at our house apart from my birthday parties. Now they were invited by my father's Kodak colleagues to dinner in the evenings, weekend barbecues and curry

28

lunches. Mummy and Daddy were very popular and soon had a large social circle. If we were not entertaining at home or invited out for Sunday lunch, we ate either at the legendary Norfolk Hotel or the Spread Eagle Hotel on the Thika road.

When they were invited out for evening meals they wrapped me in a blanket, carried me into the house and put me into somebody's bed until it was time to go home. Life was so exciting; so colourful, so comfortable; so safe, so perfect. We were such a happy family, revelling in our new life.

Our special friends who had a young daughter – also called Susan – used to take me to the drive-in cinema at Ruaraka every Sunday evening. Susan's mother, Lynn, always prepared a stew or curry which we took with us in a pressure cooker to eat at the interval. And there was always a potato in the glove pocket in case of rain. If you rubbed a cut potato on the windscreen it would repel a certain amount of water.

With the ability of a young child I soon picked up the local language, the delightfully simple Swahili, sometimes translating for my parents, explaining "*Yeye hapana jua Swahili*[5]". I don't think I consciously learned it; it just leached into my mind. I loved the language, its childlike simplicity: *tinga tinga*, tractor; *lala*, sleep, *pesi pesi*, quickly, *pole pole*, slowly.

Cinderella must have felt like this when the glass slipper fitted. I was no longer a little bundle in a liberty bodice and leggings, but a princess in pretty cotton frocks in a land of perpetual sunshine. Nairobi's climate was almost perfect, with a normal daytime temperature in the mid-70's, dropping into the 50's as night fell, which it did abruptly. There was no gentle transition; one minute it was daylight, and the next darkness. April and May generally brought welcome rain, as did November and December. As the wet seasons approached, all the talk was of whether we'd have good rains. Parched, cracked ground, dried up rivers and lakes and desperately thirsty wild animals were a horrible sight to see. When the rains did arrive, preceded by an indefinable but unmistakable smell, they did so generously, teeming onto the ground as if from a burst dam, turning dust to ankle-deep mud and pavements into flowing rivers in a matter of seconds. Apart from the occasional failure of the rains and consequent drought, the weather was reliable. When you woke up you could be almost certain that the sun would be shining. It felt to me as if I had previously been seeing the world only in monochrome, and now for the first time I was looking at it in all its wondrous colours.

Because it was the middle of the school term when we arrived, the convent where I was enrolled to continue my education could not accept me. Instead I went to Parklands school where all I can remember doing was learning times tables. All those hours of droning 'nine nines are eighty-one' must have paid off because I can still multiply up to twelve times without thinking about it. While all the other pupils wore school uniform, I was dispensed from doing so, as I would only be there for a few weeks. I stood out conspicuously, and made no friends.

Mummy thought I might enjoy the Brownies. She said we'd see how I got on before we bought the uniform. It was a wise decision. Amongst all the little girls in their baggy brown uniforms, I again looked and felt like a misfit in my pink cotton dress. As I was by nature a shy child, this did nothing for my confidence. After an hour of tying knots and rubbing tree bark, I'd had enough. I was not going to enjoy Brownies.

But these were only minor blips in a life that was otherwise as perfect as any child could wish for. There was only one really bad thing – the compulsory Sunday morning horse ride. Mummy and Daddy began taking lessons, first with John Sprague at Langata. I seem to recall that it was rather dangerous and people fell off frequently and loose horses galloped around. So they moved to a riding school run by Major Blackwell, an ex-Army officer, out towards Thika, just behind the Spread Eagle Hotel. At first, I was just a rather bored spectator, watching my parents struggling to stay aboard their mounts as they trotted bumpily in circles in the red cotton soil dust. While Major Blackwell roared from the centre of the circle: "Sit on your ARSE, not on your FANNY!" Mrs Blackwell entertained me in her kitchen and showed me her ketchup dispenser that looked like a large tomato.

Despite being bellowed at, Mummy and Daddy were enjoying the experience and suggested that I should learn to ride too. For weeks, I slumped and bounced unwillingly on the hard leather saddle, clutching desperately at the pommel. Unable to match the rhythm of the horse, I whimpered in Swahili to the African lad who ran alongside holding the reins: "Go slowly, and I'll give you a *samuni*."

"*Ndio, Memsahib Kidogo,*" he replied, maintaining his pace. This veritable ordeal was even worse because nobody realised that I was not enjoying myself. The adults imagined I was wrapped in a private cocoon of delight, while in reality I was almost speechless with terror.

We had a black dog, a part-Labrador called Pluto, and a beautiful little Persian kitten I named Minetta. She was fluffy and affectionate, and the light of my life. She understood perfectly when I explained the horrors of the weekly horse riding torment, and sighed gently in sympathy as I described each jolt and wallop.

# Chapter Four

## The Anniversary Clock

At the bungalow, Uncle Roy came to live with us as a lodger. Uncle Roy was tall and tanned with a vigorous black moustache and excellent white teeth – a Clark Gable double. He worked as a broadcaster with the British Forces Radio. I liked Uncle Roy who was jolly and sometimes mentioned my name on the radio and played a song for me. I knew Mummy liked him too, because they were often talking and laughing together. He lived with us for about three months, and then something went wrong. One evening I heard Daddy shouting at him, and Mummy was crying. Doors banged. Next morning Uncle Roy left with his suitcases. Mummy's eyes were red and swollen, and Daddy was very quiet.

At the beginning of the new school year, proudly wearing my new uniform and able to blend like a chameleon into my surroundings, I started at Loreto Convent, Valley Road. However, I have almost no recollection of school life at that time, because at home things were changing. Something very bad was happening. The magic carpet we had been riding was about to be whipped away.

There were long silences in the leather-scented car journeys to and from school. Mummy sat rigid beside my father. They didn't speak to each other. Every so often, she turned to me and talked with a forced gaiety, but something was terribly wrong. I could feel it, hear it and smell it. The horse riding lessons stopped, a huge relief for me. We didn't go out together any more. Mealtimes were uncomfortable. Often one or other of them would get up and leave the table without a word. The tension built up and up. I could feel it in my body as if I was breathing it from the air. It felt as if something was going to explode.

I can't remember what I was doing, or where I was that afternoon when my father called me into the living room and told me to sit down on the familiar chintz-upholstered settee that had come with us from England with its two matching armchairs. My father sat opposite in one of the armchairs; Mummy stood by the door.

"Your mother's going away, Sue. You have to decide who you want to be with."

This wasn't true. Of course she wasn't going away. We belonged together, the three of us. With the house, the car, Pluto and Minetta. This was our life, our family.

I sat in my own tight silence, staring first at my feet in their brown, round-toed T-bar, crepe-soled sandals with a pattern of punched-out holes in the front. I kept counting the holes where the white of my socks showed through. I counted and re-counted and looked for a message in the holes. Outside in the afternoon sun, the garden boy was watering the flowerbeds, whistling his usual monotonous tune as he splashed water onto the baked earth. On the mantelpiece sat the anniversary clock, the clock my mother and father loved and were so proud of. Its porcelain face painted with roses, it lived in a glass dome, brass balls rotating backwards and forwards as it ticked away those long seconds from our lives. It was a temperamental thing, prone to stopping at the least excuse, particularly if the surface on which it stood wasn't absolutely level. It required considerable coaxing to get going once it stopped. That clock had been such a focal point of our family life as my father fought to get the better of it, moving it around until it was satisfied, while Mummy watched anxiously.

The polished wooden floor beneath my sandals was laid in a herringbone pattern, and I moved my feet to obscure different joints. At the same time my fingers worked at the piping on the edges of the settee, rolling and squeezing it until I could see more and more of the beige cord beneath the grey fabric patterned with pink roses.

The clock ticked, the servant whistled and watered, I kept counting the holes in the sandals, gouging at the piping, and trying to hide the joints in the floorboards.

33

"Come on, Sue," said my father, "it's up to you. Make your mind up."

*Why was it up to me? How could it be?* I was nine years old. I felt a stabbing sensation in my chest, and a wave of sickness. Something was terribly wrong. I had to choose between my mother and my father. I wanted to stay with both of them, together, at the same time and in the same place. I couldn't speak; I didn't know what to say. I wanted somebody to help me.

The gardener kept whistling his whistle and the clock ticked its tick, tock and the lines between the parquet kept blurring out and my fingers picked at the piping and the number of holes in the sandals wouldn't keep still so they could be counted. Whistle, tick, whistle, tick, pick, count, recount, tick, whistle, count again. Why wouldn't the silly holes stop MOVING AROUND. Little hot tears squeezed up and out.

I sat there like a small water jug filling up and up until I finally overflowed. I had to say something, to break this terrible, painful silence. I had to choose between Mummy and Daddy, and I couldn't.

"I just want to stay here," I finally blurted out as my nose began to run. *There, I hadn't chosen anybody, had I?*

Mummy looked at me, her eyes very, very bright, then turned and walked out of the door, closing it softly behind her. Shortly afterwards a car door shut with a clunk and the sound of the engine faded as Mummy was driven away.

My father took me to Nairobi for an ice cream, but we didn't speak about what had happened. We were never going to.

*Why hadn't I shouted and cried and thrown myself on the floor, screaming that they were to stop this? Why hadn't I put up a fight instead of accepting the situation feebly? And whose idea had it been, to ask me to make such a choice?*

Decades later, I still cannot speak of that time without a painful lump rising in my throat and stifling my voice.

I went through the usual routine of washing, cleaning my teeth, going to bed, getting up, getting dressed, having breakfast cooked by the house servant, being driven to school by my father, being collected in the afternoon. In the evening, before I went to bed, we sat in the living room. My father stroked Pluto, who lay at his feet, while I cuddled Minetta.

One evening, when he came to say goodnight and turn off my light, he said: "Would you like to see your mother again, Sue?" Happy, happy, happy! She was coming back.

But no. She came and collected me to spend the weekend with her at Plums Hotel, where less than a year earlier we had arrived with such joy and anticipation of a new life. Now Mummy was sharing a *banda* with a new uncle, Uncle John. He too was an ex-RAF officer, with a flamboyant handlebar moustache, a jolly man who made a great effort to befriend me. It was all so strange. I didn't understand what was happening, or why. *When was Mummy coming back home?*

On Sunday evening Uncle John and Mummy drove me back to the bungalow. My father was waiting on the doorstep, and I was handed over, in silence.

# Chapter Five

## Gertrude's Garden

In the 1950s women could not run off with Air Force officers leaving small daughters behind without creating a scandal, especially in the incestuous expatriate community of Nairobi. Divorce was disgrace. The nuns at school were stern and unsmiling, and sniffed when they spoke to me. They made it clear they didn't approve of what our family had been getting up to. Other children talked together in huddles, looked over their shoulders and giggled. I heard the words 'divorce' and 'adultery'.

On Saturday mornings while my father was at work, I was sent back to the horrifying horse-riding lessons. Together with a group of other children, I waited on the pavement outside Kettles-Roy and Tyson, where Mummy had worked. Major Blackwell collected us in his pick-up, and after the riding ordeal delivered us back there to be collected by our parents. There was a nearby pet shop where they kept tiny crocodiles in a tank. We used to go in there and play with them.

During the months I'd been trying to learn to ride I'd made no progress at all. I lurched, rocked and thwacked about in the saddle, clinging to the pommel for grim death, bribing the African groom to go slowly, and waiting for the merciful whistle that indicated that this miserable ordeal was over for another week. Major Blackwell had accepted that he couldn't make a rider out of me, and left me to follow on as best I could. We had progressed from circling the dusty ring to going out on long hacks through the African scrub. Major Blackwell led us in procession, me inevitably bringing up the rear on a sleepy pony. At certain points he would raise his hand in the air

36

and call "Trot on!" and the automatic horses would break into the pace, the other children rising and falling in perfect rhythm with their mounts while I thumped clumsily. And suddenly, one day, I could do it. I could rise and sit, rise and sit, perfectly, and I called out triumphantly: "Major Blackwell, look, I can trot!"

I was so overwhelmed by this achievement that I was waving both arms in the air, reins around the horse's legs. "So you can," he replied in disbelief, and after that there was no looking back.

Soon I could canter and jump small obstacles, with no stirrups and arms crossed, thanks to the major's military method of teaching – a tight knee-grip made for a safe seat. That was the riding style taught then – short stirrups and knees clamped like limpets to the saddle; depth of seat would come later. Once in a while we had brief, exhilarating full-tilt gallops over the plains and I felt that there was nothing I couldn't do as long as I was on horseback. The weekly nightmare became my greatest joy. I lived day and night for the time I would be in the creaking saddle with the smell of hot horse sweat in my nose, the shiny mane-hair and pricked ears ahead, and the red dust engrained in my skin, clothing and hair. And for those couple of hours I could push to the back of my mind the fact that Mummy had left.

Then I started having hay fever, which was particularly aggravated by the lantana bush, which grew in abundance around the area where we rode. I sneezed and wheezed continually, and my eyes itched until I rubbed them raw and they swelled shut. The doctor prescribed antihistamines that sent me to sleep at my desk or on horseback. And then my fingers started to itch. They itched so badly that I scratched them raw, and weaved a handkerchief in between them and then pulled it really hard, again and again to stop the terrible irritation. Shiny, tiny watery blisters covered both hands, burning and prickling and leaking clear fluid from them. The sweat and dust aggravated my skin beyond endurance as the tiny blisters merged into each other and burst, then turned yellow; my fingers swelled up like chipolatas until I couldn't bend them, the skin cracked and oozed. I hid this from my father in case he stopped me from riding. I think that he was immersed so deeply in his unhappiness at the time that he noticed very little. No matter that I could barely hold a pencil at school, or a knife and fork, I could still pinch the reins between the tips of my fingers and guide the horse with my legs and voice, and that was all that mattered.

But after several weeks my hands were a swollen raw mass of yellow oozing cracks that itched furiously but were agony to scratch. Even water burned them. I couldn't hide it any longer and my father whisked me off to the doctor. He diagnosed acute eczema, and that afternoon I was admitted to Gertrude's Garden, the children's hospital founded by Colonel Grogan in the affluent Muthaiga suburb of Nairobi.

During the ten days I stayed there, Mummy visited daily, as did my father. They came at different times so that they didn't collide. I've no idea what treatment I had, and my sole recollection of the place was endless meals of warm semolina sprinkled with coloured sugar. When I came home, horse riding was off the menu.

The next time I saw my mother was a few weeks later, when we went together by coach on holiday to Mombasa. While we were there Mummy told me that she and Uncle John were going to be married shortly and then they would go to live in South Africa. Once they had moved, we wouldn't see each other for a while because South Africa was very far away, but Mummy would always love me.

*How long was a while? How far was far away?* I was too afraid to ask because I feared the answers.

Kenya's State of Emergency was at its height. However likeable the house servants, they couldn't be trusted. Some had been forced to take hideous oaths of loyalty to the Mau Mau who were notorious for the appalling cruelty with which they treated their victims. Breaking of those oaths meant certain terrible death. Many thousands of loyal Africans were murdered by the Mau Mau, and a few dozen Europeans, among whom two young boys had been butchered very near Major Blackwell's riding school. When Europeans talked of the terrorists, as they were then regarded, they called them 'Mickey Mouse'. A suspect had been shot running from the police across the arid patch of grass at the bottom of our garden.

Early one evening, my father came in to my bedroom and said he

38

had to tell me something. From his sad face it was obviously not going to be good news.

Working five and a half days a week, he couldn't look after me during the school holidays. Nor could he leave me at home with the servant at this dangerous time. So I was to go back to England to boarding school. During the school holidays I would live with my paternal grandparents whom I barely knew. I was leaving in a week's time.

Before I left, we went to Nairobi's largest toyshop to choose something to take with me. There was a donkey, a Merrythought soft toy with a gigantic head and ears, disproportionately small body and legs, and a little red plastic saddle and bridle. It was love at first sight, but I saw the price tag and selected something more modest. My father picked up the donkey and said: "Wouldn't you rather have this fellow? I think he'd like you to be his owner. Shall we get him?" And so we did, and I christened him Flicker, after my favourite pony at Major Blackwell's riding school.

The night before I left, my father came into my room and talked to me about the new school I would be going to. There were ponies; my aunt would visit me and Granny would look after me in the holidays. Probably it wouldn't be too long before I could come back home. Then he burst into tears and held me and rocked me, weeping and sobbing. I felt it wasn't so much for me and my departure but for my mother who had left that he grieved so terribly.

And it is only as I write that I recall that was the only time I ever saw him express any strong feeling. That makes me sad, almost tearful as I recognise that he wasn't capable of displaying emotion. Maybe that explains many of the things that were to come.

With Flicker clamped firmly under my arm, I followed a stewardess across the tarmac at Nairobi's Eastleigh airport to board a BOAC Comet, turning to see my father waving from the departure lounge window. The Comet was notorious for its poor safety record, but fortunately I didn't know that then. Even if I had, it would probably not have alarmed me. I was in an emotional vacuum, numbed by all that had happened so quickly, and life had a trance-like quality. I had not cried since Mummy left. I didn't seem to have any tears left.

The plane taxied, accelerated and bounced into the sky. A steward wheeled a trolley down the aisle, carving roast beef individually for each passenger, and heaping the china plates with carrots, roast potatoes, cabbage and gravy. There was ice cream and fruit salad for dessert. Long after the other passengers' plates had been cleared away, I was still contentedly chewing. Cheap flights, package holidays, pre-packed shrink-wrapped meals were unheard of. Air travel then was luxurious and elegant. In the ladies' toilets I watched a woman raiding the racks of Cyclax skin products – toner, freshener, moisturiser and scent, busily decanting them into her own little jars in a vanity case.

"Well, dear," she explained, "after all, we do pay for it."

The flight wasn't without incident. Coming in to land in Rome the landing gear would not descend and the plane slithered gratingly along the runway on its metal belly, coming to a halt amid showers of golden sparks, shudders and rasping noises. My neighbour in the adjacent seat was a fatherly American gentleman who kindly shepherded Flicker and me around the airport during the subsequent delay of several hours. He bought me my first Neapolitan ice cream.

Our arrival in England was far later than scheduled, and then the plane was diverted from Heathrow to Gatwick due to thick fog. I suppose somebody must have got me onto a train to Victoria station, where my two grandmothers were waiting for me. Nan I recognised instantly; Granny was a stranger. Swathed in a choking yellow-grey miasma of smog, the noxious marriage of fog and coal smoke, we groped our way to a Lyons Corner House where we drank tea and ate cherry tarts. The two grandmothers treated each other with the exquisite politeness peculiar to people who hate each other. Then Nan went back to her bed-sit in Wimbledon while Granny and I took the bus to my new home in Thirsk Road, Lavender Hill, Clapham Junction.

We felt our way from the bus stop and along the railings, breathing the cold thickness of the air, until we reached the terraced Victorian house that was going to be my new part-time home for the foreseeable future.

The front door with its stained-glass window led via a long, dark linoleumed corridor into a small room, cosily heated by a coal fire. Next to the fire sat a very small man who gave a brief grunt. There was a budgerigar cage on a sideboard. Pushed against one wall was a small dining table covered with a crocheted cloth. I sat in a chair by the fireplace, facing the grunter.

"Take your shoes off and warm your feet up," Granny said, and went into the kitchen to make me a hot drink. The grandfather in the other chair remained silent and impassive, staring at the coals. I sat with Flicker squeezed under my arm, pointing my feet at the flames and drinking a cup of sweetened milk. When the cup was empty, Granny said that it was bedtime and I should follow her. As I went obediently through the door into the chilly corridor, a snappy little voice called:

"Oi, you. Get back here and pick your shoes up! There's no little black boys here to run around after you."

Actually, Granddad, horrible little shit that you were, there never had been any little black boys running around after me. I picked up the shoes and followed Granny, thinking that life here wasn't going to be quite all I might wish.

# Chapter Six

# Clapham Junction

Granddad had a single endearing feature: the permanent collection of black and white circular bird droppings that sat on the bald space amongst the wispy grey hair still clinging to his nasty old head. A tiny wizened man, he sat shrivelled in the small chair beside the fire, a permanent sneer on his face, suspicious little darting eyes and a minuscule, skinny cigarette glued to his bottom lip, with shreds of tobacco peeking from its end. He was nothing like the kindly old man in the cardigan in the Werther's advertisement feeding caramels to his little grandson.

A blue budgerigar, whose name was Joey, lived in and around the cage on the sideboard. His favourite perch was on Granddad's head, where he deposited his neat little offerings. Hurray for Joey! I'd have liked to play with Joey and make a fuss of him, but when I held out my hand to him, Granddad snarled: "Leave him alone. The bird don't want you messing about with it."

Granddad always wore dark trousers held up with braces over a collarless shirt, and looked as if he needed to shave more thoroughly. When he wasn't scrunched in the chair he was out fishing. He never brought his catch home but tipped it back into the canal from where he'd wrenched it. It seemed to me a pointless pastime, and unnecessarily traumatic for the fish, particularly to be caught by him, but at least it got him out of the chair and away from the house for a while.

Granny's name was Lizzie. Not Elizabeth. Lizzie. She had pierced ears because, she said, it improved your eyesight. She was taller and broader than her husband, with faded wiry yellow hair and a shapeless amiable face that looked as if somebody had sat on it before it was quite set. Her voice was gurgly and she had a perpetual cough, the result of excessive smoking. Her daily pleasure was a small bottle of stout bought from the off-licence on the corner of the street. Once in a while, when she sent me to collect it she gave me a few pennies for a bottle of Tizer. She was good-natured with a ribald sense of humour, breaking wind fairly frequently and uninhibitedly, then asking in a loud voice: "Who's let Johnny out of prison?" I found this embarrassing, as it was not at all the sort of thing that had been done, or had certainly never been mentioned, by my parents. Sometimes she would reminisce: "Oh, you should have seen me on my wedding day, with my beautiful golden hair hanging right down to my bum." I could easily see her as a glamorous blonde bride, but I couldn't imagine Granddad, whose name was Jim, anything other than an embittered, hunched up little man.

Granny never volunteered any information about herself or her upbringing, but she would always laugh when she remembered times when her children were small and naughty and she'd send them to the hardware shop to buy a cane with which to beat them. By the time they came back (and it could be many hours later), she would have forgotten what they'd done, and instead of beating them would blow bubbles of spit through the cane to amuse them.

She and Granddad owned the mid-terrace, three-storey Victorian house and lived on the ground floor. The first floor was rented to an elderly meek couple who crept up and down the stairs when they came in and went out. Granddad kept a broom beside his chair so that he could thump the ceiling at the slightest noise from the lodgers as they moved about or opened and closed doors.

On the top floor of the house two rooms had been carefully and attractively decorated to make quarters for me, a bedroom and a playroom where I could entertain myself. The walls were papered with tiny pink roses and the windows curtained to match; it really did look very pretty. Unfortunately, I was absolutely terrified up there, at the top of the house, far from anybody else. This was the bedroom, in fact the very bed where my great aunt Maggie had died. I still had a clear image from our visit before we left to go to Kenya

43

of the gaunt, dark-haired woman with a lined, yellowing face and hacking cough. Nothing could convince me that her ghost was not lurking malevolently in the menacing, dark wardrobe, rather like Mr Beeblesticks, ready to pounce the moment I closed my eyes. So I rocked from side to side through the night, wide-eyed and rigid with fear.

Great-aunt Maggie wasn't the only imagined threat. I had a further anxiety: teddy boys. This was their era, when Bill Haley's *Rock Around the Clock* was taking the teenagers by storm. They rocked and jived in the aisles of the cinemas with their hair greased into pompadours, wearing drainpipe trousers, long black jackets, shoestring ties and thick crepe-soled shoes. From the pulpits, priests preached the end of civilisation as we knew it. My fear was that a teddy boy would climb in through the sash window that opened out onto the roofs of houses in the next row, and cut my throat. Just why I thought this, I've no idea, but with all the adverse attention they were attracting, they'd made a powerful impression upon me.

After a week of sleepless nights and days filled with fear at the prospect of another isolated night on the second floor, I confessed to Granny that I was frightened up there. From then on I took up nocturnal residence downstairs on a large cold green leather settee that lived in what was called "the front room." It was dark and gloomy at night, but at least I felt safe, watched over by two large bronze statues of nearly-naked men holding rearing horses on the mantelpiece. It wasn't an ideal bedroom, as a grandfather clock stood in the corridor outside, lugubriously banging out the hour, half-hour and quarter-hour, preceded by a series of pinging and whirring noises. Granddad spat his contempt at my feebleness, but although I was often sleepless I wasn't afraid. The bed was never warm, even during the summer. In the winter, Granny put in a stone hot water bottle that heated a small area of the sheets. By morning, it would be icy cold.

There was no bathroom downstairs; the lodgers had the benefit of that up on the landing between the first and second floors, together with the only indoor lavatory. Our convenience lived in a concrete shed in a small paved yard to the rear of the house, next to the bomb shelter. We washed, and cleaned our teeth in the kitchen sink. A large zinc bathtub hung from a hook behind the kitchen door. One night each week, Granny lugged it into the living room and placed in front of the fire, then filled it from kettles of hot water. There was something comforting and homely about sitting in the tub with the flames jumping up the chimney. One side was much warmer than the other, and the water could have benefited from being deeper, but it is still one of my fonder memories of life on Lavender Hill.

Granny didn't have any labour-saving devices – no vacuum cleaner, washing machine, dishwasher or refrigerator. She scrubbed the doorstep to blinding whiteness on her knees, using a galvanised bucket, scrubbing brush and block of soap. She washed the laundry in a copper vat of boiling water, mashing it around with a wooden paddle, scrubbing it on a wooden washboard then squeezing the excess water out through the hand-driven rollers of a mangle – a lengthy and back-breaking task. The mangled laundry was hung on a line to dry in the back yard, or, if it was raining as it mostly seemed to be, over a wooden frame in the front room before the coal fire. Once the sheets were dry, they had to be pulled by their corners by two people, snapped and jerked to remove as many creases as possible, and folded before moving to the ironing pile. Before ironing she inspected them, and if they were worn at the centre, she cut them down the middle and sewed them back together with the outer edges to the centre to give them a fresh lease of life. Then they'd be laboriously and perfectly ironed, and thoroughly aired on the rack in front of the fire before being laid to rest. Laundry took up all of Granny's Monday.

Frozen vegetables, supermarkets, food processors and convenience meals were things of the future. Shopping trips were made on foot from one shop to the next, with a shopping basket or string bag. Granny and her cronies always had time to stop and gossip, their arms stretched long from decades of carrying heavy loads, and their hands rough and red. The old ladies met on their shopping trips and chattered cheerfully on the cold pavements, in their south London voices. They talked about people I didn't and would never know, and things I didn't understand while I shuffled from one bored foot to another. They all looked worn out, but never suffered from stress or nervous breakdowns.

In a drawer on the dresser, Granny kept a green and yellow tube of a pleasant-smelling slimy stuff called Glymiel Jelly that she massaged into her poor old hands, and a white chalky pencil she ran beneath her fingernails to whiten them. When she wasn't shopping, cooking or doing her household chores, she sat contentedly knitting (often using my upraised arms to wind the skeins of wool into neat balls), or crocheting while she listened to the radio, occasionally adding a few chunks of coke to the fire.

She prepared delicious, cheap and nourishing working class food: eels bought from our local fishmonger, where they writhed in shallow white enamel pans. Once at home, she nonchalantly decapitated them and tossed the heads into the fire. They squirmed interestingly and gruesomely for a few minutes before charring away to nothing, while the bodies were cooked into pies. And she cooked the soggy face-flannel stuff called tripe into an exquisite meal coated in a thick creamy onion sauce. Boiled mutton with caper sauce, steak and kidney pies and puddings weeping mahogany-coloured gravy, fragrant liver and onions: these were the meals Granny served and which I can still smell and taste. Bread or crumpets were toasted over the fire on the end of a long brass toasting fork and thickly slathered with butter.

On Saturday mornings, we walked to Battersea Rise and bought pints of shrimps or winkles from the market for afternoon tea. Using a darning needle to spiral the winkles out of their shells, we dipped them in vinegar and ate them with brown bread and butter. Often I'd find minute hermit crabs in the shells, and put them carefully into jam jars of water, despite being told that they were dead because they'd been boiled alive. I always hoped that maybe one day one would miraculously survive. Sometimes Granny bought whelks, but I couldn't eat them – I thought they looked like Granddad's toes would look if he took off his socks. Once I took one of the small 'feet' from a winkle and stuck it to my face, mimicking the beauty spot that Mummy used to draw beside her mouth. From the armchair by the fire, Granddad growled: "Get that off your face, you." I think

46

it reminded him of her, too.

Remembering those days I find myself a little misty-eyed, and I wonder why. I was not happy there, nor unhappy; I was just there. Maybe it's just the memory of a time when life in general was simple that brings a wave of nostalgia.

Two of the most noticeable differences between Nairobi and Clapham Junction were the trees and birds. In Clapham Junction there was no pale blue jacaranda, no glowing orange Nandi flames, nor tall shimmering eucalyptus, pink and white oleanders, rustling pepper trees, acacias or whistling thorns, and no magical, sweet-smelling Yesterday Today and Tomorrow plants – their blossoms which had been indigo yesterday were pale blue today, and would be white by tomorrow. In Clapham Junction there weren't any trees at all. Only tarmac, bricks and concrete and long periods of freezing weather and endless rain. A monochrome world. To see grass and trees, we walked to Clapham Common or Battersea Gardens.

Sometimes a pigeon flew onto the roof of the bomb shelter, or a couple of sparrows bopped around picking up crumbs. They were drab creatures after the magnificence of glossy starlings and hummingbirds whose metallic sheen flashed in the sunlight as they probed the hearts of flowers, the furry feathered mousebirds or the yellow weaver birds whose warren-like network of nests festooned the thorn trees. There wasn't really very much natural colour at all in Clapham Junction.

My father had two sisters, both slightly eccentric and funny, and more exuberant and confident than their brother. Auntie Veronica was tall and fairly slim with a penetrating, theatrical voice. As she had over-plucked her eyebrows and they no longer grew, she drew on two high-arched replicas with a thick brown pencil. This gave her a permanently astonished expression; not helped by a perforated grey rubber garment called a roll-on which she struggled into every day so that her stomach and backside were squashed in flat. She lived in Mitcham with her gorgeous husband. A big good-natured man with a deep voice, Uncle Arthur was nearly always laughing. He was modestly successful, the Managing Director of a small company manufacturing vacuum cleaner spare parts, and he was an

47

excellent pianist.

Auntie Elspeth was much smaller than her sister, birdlike in fact, with the abundant energy that those teeny people often have. That was just as well, because her husband, Uncle Ratty, never lifted a finger to do anything at all, not even drive his car, a huge Rover. It was before the days of power steering, and doll-sized Auntie Elspeth had to sit on two cushions to see over the steering wheel, struggling to reach the pedals with her short legs and little feet. It was a dreadful battle for her to manoeuvre the vehicle into tight spaces. She sat white-knuckled, tight-lipped and sweating as she strained to get the car where Uncle Ratty told her. Meanwhile he sat in it looking irritated and disapproving. A change from his normally smug, self-satisfied expression that reflected the fact that generally he got everything he wanted and was a far more successful person than anybody else he knew.

Uncle Ratty looked like a giant pixie. He was one of the top men at a household-name company in the Far East. He and the small aunt had spent most of their married life in Singapore and Kuala Lumpur. Their older daughter, Marilyn, was sophisticated and attractive and had married a wealthy English businessman. They lived with their two boys in Singapore, a glamorous and apparently united life. Some years later, the perfect husband began uniting with a succession of beautiful Chinese girls. Cousin Marilyn emerged from her divorce with her reputation untarnished and married an older, quieter and less flighty but even wealthier gentleman.

Her sister Jennifer was six months younger than me. Because of her rebellious and unpredictable behaviour she was regarded as a terror. Her parents had sent her back from Asia to live with Auntie Veronica. I don't know exactly what she did, but from conversations I overheard between Granny and Auntie Veronica she was a source of real torment and anxiety to them. She had a particularly wild streak and was cheeky, bolder and far less inhibited than I was. As she was at a local day school they had little rest from her, but despite that they were very fond of her and even Granddad grunted at her occasionally. The fact that he was as unwelcoming towards his two daughters as he was to me was of some comfort, and made me feel a

48

little less personally responsible for his unpleasantness. When they came to visit he grunted when they greeted him, and returned to his newspaper. He was marginally friendlier towards Jennifer. He didn't hug her and offer her a toffee, but he used to say when she arrived: "Oh, you're here again."

Granny enjoyed playing cards and board games with Jennifer and myself. On wet afternoons we sat at the dining table tossing dice, sliding plastic buttons up and down snakes and ladders and inexpertly dealing cards. However Granny was a blatant and completely unrepentant cheat and sometimes reduced me to tears of frustration as she tricked her way to a string of cackled self-congratulatory victories. Although only 56 years old, she was already a worn out and tired old lady and with a silent husband who didn't do anything apart from sitting reading the paper or going fishing. Granny even had to haul the buckets of coal and coke up from the cellar while he sat reading the paper. After raising three children of her own, having the responsibility for a small introverted girl must have placed an unwelcome burden on her.

I ought not to have been a very great liability to Granny, but somehow I knew that I was. I was quiet and obedient, ate everything she gave me as fast as I was able and amused myself for long hours. My awful bouncy, springy all-over-the-place hair was the bane of my life. If, when it was wet I thumped it down firmly and tied it down tightly under a nylon scarf, it would when dry remain flat and manageable for about an hour. During that time I looked a little less like Struwwelpeter after a hurricane. One evening my hair was still damp at bedtime, and Granny told me to get a towel and rub it dry. *Can you imagine what it was going to look like?* I asked if I could keep the nylon scarf on it during the night. She put both hands to her head and wailed: "Oh God, what have I done to deserve all this?" and burst into tears. I realised I was the 'all this,' but wondered whether she wasn't rather over-reacting because I wanted to sleep with a scarf on my head. Poor Granny.

She looked after me as best she could. Nan spoiled and loved me. The reciprocal loathing of the two sides of the family was like a blast of icy wind. Painstakingly polite exchanges emphasised the fact that they would each as soon have been chewing wasps. I would never know what made the two sides of the family so hostile towards each other. Certainly my parent's divorce hadn't helped, but even before we went to Africa I could only remember visiting my father's parents once, so there was a longer-standing reason for the rift.

Between my two grandmothers was a wide social divide. Nan came from a family who had been financially comfortable. She was beautifully spoken and rigidly correct, and if she had a fault it was her intolerance of modern music, clothes and behaviour. She would no more have farted publicly, or said 'bum' than she would have eaten burning coals. She lived according to the Victorian standards by which she had grown up, and was never willing, or maybe able to accept a more modern approach to life. Once a week during the school holidays she came to collect me from Thirsk Road. I would hear a single rap on the door, and walking down the gloomy corridor I could see her wavy shape through the front's door stained glass window, where she stood patiently and with dignity on Granny's scrubbed white doorstep.

When she died she left me a plastic envelope containing various family papers, a family tree drawn on crinkly blue airmail paper, and a number of notes about people, places and events in her life. The first passage in her notes reads:

> *'My grandmother had a lovely pink and white complexion – with almost a peach-like down – but certainly clear and young for her years – and to what did she attribute this – nothing but her own urine. She would dip a towel into the chamber pot and dab it on her face. I was horrified lest she should expect me to do the same – it was a secret which I never told until I was much older and could discuss my grandmother with my parents. Grandma said that all foreign women did this, and it may be so, because of course during her singing career she had met and worked with women singers of all nations.'*

Despite her grandmother's unconventional beauty routine and her own divorce, Nan was a model of middle-class Victorian rectitude, while Granny was scruffily cheery and harmlessly vulgar. Her dour little husband had been a butcher and came originally from Scotland. I expect Scotland was heartily glad to see the back of him. Paradoxically, it was Granny and Granddad who owned their own home, which you could buy these days for around £600,000, while Nan lived modestly in rented accommodation and had no money of her own apart from her salary.

On cold wet days we went to the cinema or stayed in her little bed-sit in Wimbledon doing jigsaw puzzles and feeding sixpenny pieces into the gas fire to keep warm. In the summer she took me to zoos, museums, parks and for pony rides. With Nan and her friends I was a nice little girl whom they enjoyed fussing over and kissing with biscuit-flavoured breath. With Granny, I always felt a vague sense of disapproval, as if I was in some way to blame for the unfortunate circumstances which had brought me to this dismal environment. Granny's friends scrutinised me as you might regard a suspected bed-bug. But I didn't care – I had Flicker, plenty of books and the dream of going back home to Kenya to my father, Pluto and Minetta. I lived inside my head, wondering where my mother was and whether I'd ever see her again.

Each year at Christmas, Nan took me to a London show or pantomime, but Christmas Day was spent with my father's branch of the family, normally at Auntie Veronica and Uncle Arthur's house in Mitcham, where an awful painting of a long-necked woman with blue skin hung over the tiled mantelpiece around the gas fire. They were jolly events, and after our meal we sang along to Uncle Arthur playing his prized piano in the front room.

When Uncle Ratty retired, he returned from the Far East with the small aunt to live in England in a rather beautiful house in desirable Old Coulsdon. Jennifer grudgingly moved in with her parents to make their life as hateful as she could. That year the whole family was invited for Christmas lunch. I'll never forget Christmas day there.

Auntie Elspeth came in the car to collect me from Thirsk Road on Christmas Eve, so that I could help with decorating the tree. Auntie Veronica and Uncle Arthur, Granny and Granddad would join us the following day.

Jennifer and I shared a room, listening to pop music from the pirate ship Radio Caroline long into the night. Uncle Ratty had issued strict orders that on no account whatsoever were we to get up and disturb him too early next morning. After waking we lay in bed whispering and giggling until 9.00 am, which we hoped was not too early for Uncle Ratty. Sure enough he was up, and sitting reading warmly and comfortably at the breakfast table.

It had snowed heavily that night, quite unusual for snow to fall as early as Christmas day. Outside was a perfect picture postcard scene, complete with a robin bouncing around by the doorstep. From the kitchen window we could see a succession of deep tracks leading from the front door to a small building about twenty yards down the garden. Auntie Elspeth was struggling up the path with a laden galvanised coal scuttle. She was less than five feet tall, and the snow was well above her ankles. The fireplace was large and it took her several journeys to fill the brass coal box that sat on the hearth, while Uncle Ratty continued reading. When he paused to look up once or twice at his wife's exertions, there was a smile of absolute contentment on his big pixie face. Jennifer and I decided we would go and help, and started pulling on our boots.

"Sit down. She doesn't need help," he growled. "She can manage perfectly well." He pulled the newspaper to his face, while Jennifer and I stuck out our tongues at him.

By the time the coal box was filled to his satisfaction, he was ready for his breakfast. The little auntie cooked up fried bread, sausages, bacon, grilled mushrooms and tomatoes and fried egg. It seemed a very hearty breakfast considering we would be eating a large Christmas meal a few hours later, but like the coal box Uncle Ratty took a lot of satisfying.

Jennifer asked if we could open our presents.

"When I've finished my breakfast. Just sit still and be patient." He worked his way in a leisurely manner around his plate, pausing from time to time to sip delicately from his coffee cup, and pushing it towards the auntie to indicate that it needed replenishing. When at last his plate and cup were empty, Jennifer stood up and said she was going to open her presents – by then the wall clock indicated that it was almost 10.30am.

"SIT DOWN!" he roared. "I haven't finished. *I'll* tell you when it's time." Jennifer flopped down, glaring at him.

"Toast."

Auntie Elspeth popped two slices of bread into the toaster. When they hopped up to the top, she carefully buttered them and placed them in front of him. Very slowly, possibly because he was not used to lifting a finger for himself, but probably just to prolong our wait, he applied a thin coat of marmalade, spreading it evenly over the surface, smoothing out any lumps, making sure it went right to the edges and into the corners. After cutting each slice into two neat triangles, he pushed his coffee cup for another refill, and started chewing very, very slowly. I don't know what the aunt felt, but Jennifer and I sat there hating him, willing him to choke to death. When he had demolished the toast, he ordered a further two slices which Auntie Elspeth obediently prepared. Finally, just before 11.00am he said we could open our presents.

I had a satisfying stack of fancy-paper-wrapped gifts, thanks to the generosity of both aunts, an incomparable improvement on the customarily disappointing little stocking that was Granny's best offering. Jennifer's present was a very large leather suitcase tightly packed with clothes. Beautiful clothes, beautiful underwear, fabulous shoes. A whole magnificent wardrobe of outfits.

"Now, young lady, I want to see you looking smart when our guests arrive," said her father. The neighbourhood notables were invited for sherry and mince pies at mid-day. Silently Jennifer pulled everything out of the case until it lay in a colourful and expensive pile in the middle of the floor. Then she walked out of the room. I followed her to the bedroom we shared, where she was rummaging through a wardrobe and drawers, pulling out heaps of drab and raggedy clothes.

"What are you going to wear?"

"Don't know yet," she replied, riffling through her wardrobe filled with expensive and lovely outfits, but she was concentrating on the tatters.

53

"What about all those fantastic new clothes you just got?" I asked. She shrugged. "What about them?"

When the first guests started arriving, Auntie Elspeth put her head round the door and called: "Come on you two, show yourselves!"

Jennifer still hadn't chosen anything to wear, so I left her and went in to the lounge to pass around sausage rolls, cocktail sausages and warm mince pies.

"Where's Jennifer?" asked Uncle Ratty.

"She's getting dressed."

It was a lively affair with lots of guffawing, cigar smoke, chinking glasses and tinkling laughter, Uncle Ratty was the perfect charming host; the flames flickered in the fireplace and the snowflakes piled up outside. Auntie Elspeth was a very extrovert character who habitually dressed in red. Today she wore a tight-fitting scarlet dress with very high-heeled black shoes, and she smoked Sobranie cocktail cigarettes in pastel colours. She announced that she had been learning some kind of martial art which made her immune to pain. There were no takers for her request to have a lighted cigarette pressed into the palm of her hand, so instead she prostrated herself in the middle of the floor and insisted that everybody in the room should take it in turns to stand on her stomach. There she lay, a tiny birdlike thing, while one by one we took off our shoes and stood balanced on her belly, while she laughed and said it didn't hurt.

When Jennifer made her entrance, conversation stopped for a moment. She was dressed in a shapeless dark brown nylon pinafore dress over a blue shiny pyjama top. Her legs were shrouded in brown nylon stockings full of ladders, and she had on scuffed brown shoes. Her thick dark hair was scrunched up into odd bunches. Her very large dark eyes were smudged with quantities of thick black make-up giving her the appearance of a sad panda, and her lipstick was pale pink, almost white. She looked like a refugee who got to the clothing queue after everybody else. Uncle Ratty's face was a gratifying picture of rage. He went quite purple, but Jennifer just smiled and walked into the crowd around her horizontal mother. I envied her confidence.

Thinking back now, I realise that I was not the only one in the

54

family with issues.

The gathering broke up after an hour and a half, and at 2.00pm Granny and Granddad arrived for lunch with Auntie Veronica and Uncle Arthur. How my tiny aunt managed single-handedly to cope with her horrid husband, cook breakfast, haul coal, prepare the trays of titbits for the drinks party and then put such a spectacular meal on the table, heaven knows. She never lost her serene smile and air of being perfectly in control. The contrast between life in the Far East where they had lived in splendour with a team of servants must have been enormous, but she seemed to take everything effortlessly in her small stride.

The table was set beautifully with bone china crockery, silver cutlery and crystal wine glasses. Candles burned in silver candlesticks, garlands and swags of holly and ivy twined down the table around expensive golden crackers. The meal started with a silver tureen of asparagus soup with crisp bread rolls and creamy butter. We pulled the crackers and donned silly paper hats, even the grunter wore one, and we drank the best wine from the beautiful glasses; Jennifer and I were allowed a single glass. Refusing any help, Auntie Elspeth cleared the soup course and wheeled in a hostess trolley bearing a chubby golden-skinned turkey; roast potatoes; creamed potatoes; roasted parsnips; Brussels sprouts; baby carrots; minted peas; crispy bacon rolls; shiny chipolata sausages; cranberry sauce; bread sauce; gravy and two types of stuffing. There were oohs! and aahs! and much smacking of lips. The grunter snorted.

She placed the turkey ceremoniously in front of Uncle Ratty. You may find it a little unusual that he was going to do something as energetic as carving, but I think it was to demonstrate his position as lord of all he surveyed. Like a surgeon, he signalled for the carving knife and fork, which the aunt dutifully slapped into his hands. He carved a perfect slice of breast which he laid carefully on a plate that was passed to Granny. As he carved we passed bowl after bowl of vegetables and sauces around the table.

Then the telephone rang.

He answered it and spoke in a low voice for a few moments while we heaped our plates and laughed. Suddenly there was a crash. The plates and glasses jumped and rattled, wine slopped and peas rolled onto the cloth as Uncle Ratty's fist smashed onto the table. He bellowed: "SHUT UP, you bloody people! Just shut up! I'm trying to talk to my mother."

He spat towards his wife: "Your bloody parents are here, in my house, eating my food and drinking my wine, while my mother is down there in Christchurch. Now just bloody well keep quiet while I talk to her."

We all laid our cutlery down gingerly on our plates and sat in deathly, unmoving silence while he talked for about 10 minutes. When he put the receiver down he stalked silently out of the room. We didn't see him again that day. Just as well he had eaten the hearty breakfast to keep him going.

"Come on, everyone, eat up before it gets cold!" chirped Auntie Elspeth brightly. We tried to finish the meal she had cooked so carefully, and tried to keep a cheerful conversation alive. We struggled through the flaming Christmas pudding, brandy butter, cream and custard, and even forced down a mince pie and a glass of cherry brandy. But we were a very subdued and uncomfortable gathering, and as soon as they could the guests prepared to leave. I was scheduled to stay for a few more days, but when Granny asked if I would like to go home with them, I did. That was Christmas day at Uncle Ratty's.

But the small aunt could be pretty weird, too. Uncle Ratty's parents lived in south Hampshire in a magnificent house with a large garden. They were the sweetest, kindest people. How they had spawned something quite as hateful as Uncle Ratty is hard to imagine. Jennifer and I went to stay there for a fortnight's holiday with Auntie Elspeth. Old Mr Hatfield grew all their fruit and vegetables and his wife made jams and pies and cakes and biscuits, and spoiled us wonderfully.

At the time, Jennifer and I were closely bonded in cousinly love, which wasn't always the case. We found a tiny dead shrew, mourned it, and buried it encased in a pea-pod which her kindly old grandfather supplied. A local shopkeeper upset us. I don't remember why, but we trapped wasps in a jam jar, pushed them into a matchbox and posted it through the man's letterbox. On reflection we felt this was insufficient retribution, so we got another matchbox and placed in it a portion of dog shit, and posted him that, too.

Although I didn't have quite such difficulty in swallowing as I had earlier, I was still a slow eater. Long after everyone else had finished eating and was starting to think about the next meal, I'd still be chomping on the main course. The atmosphere in this household was relaxed and comfortable, and nobody seemed to mind sitting chatting at the table while I battled with my food. One lunch time while I was churning the last of my creamed potatoes around and around, I happened to look at my dessert. A bowl of blackberries freshly-picked from the garden, smothered in thick yellow cream. Everybody else had long since finished their meal. The blackberries were a rich purple colour that leached swirling streams of pink into the cream, and I studied this as I tried to swallow. I was certain I could see movement in the cream. I looked closer. The surface was rapidly filling with tiny black wriggly things that swam around until they made it to the edge of the cream lake, and then started hauling their little bodies up the side of the bowl. I glanced up and met my aunt's amused grin as I gulped down the last mouthful of potato.

"There's a good girl," said Jennifer's gentle grandmother. "Now you have some lovely blackberries and cream – they'll go down nice and easily."

I pleaded being too full, being too tired, but while the old lady said that was fine, of course I didn't have to eat them, the little auntie was determined to see me eat the bowl of maggots.

She wouldn't accept any excuse I could think of. Auntie Elspeth was adamant. Finally there was nothing left to do but cry, "But there are little things in it! Little creatures crawling in the cream and climbing up the side of the bowl!"

The old lady looked horrified and peered at the bowl. "Well," she said doubtfully, "I can't see anything, dear. But you just leave it if you don't want it."

"Don't be so silly, Susan," laughed my aunt. "They're just part of the blackberries! Do you think Nanny Hatfield would give you food that had things in it? Now eat it up before I start to get cross."

So I spooned the blackberries and cream and little maggots into my mouth and managed to swallow them. Then I went to the bathroom and was sick.

Years later, I reminded my aunt of this incident. She tilted back her head and roared with laughter. "Yes, I remember those maggots. They'd obviously come out of the blackberries and got into the cream because your bowl had been sitting there for so long. But I thought to myself, well, I've eaten them, and so has everybody else, so why shouldn't you?" It seemed to me a rather inadequate reason to make a child eat a bowl of maggots, but as I said, she was a bit weird.

Jennifer really was angry with her mother over this affair. Whether it was a purely partisan feeling towards me because we were so friendly at that time, or whether because she realised she'd eaten maggots too, but she insisted that her mother should be punished. We came up with a simple but satisfyingly successful sentence. Auntie Elspeth was paralysed by fear of spiders, even tiny ones. After an abortive attempt to hunt and catch something that would really scare her, we improvised. Each of our beds had on it a woolly plaid blanket with a black fringe. We cut off pieces of the fringe, knotted them into quite realistic-looking thick spiders, and put them in her bed between the sheets. That evening we lay giggling quietly, waiting impatiently for the door of her bedroom to close. Two minutes later, her piercing shriek of pure, absolute terror was a joy to hear.

# Chapter Seven

# The Surrey Hills

I've jumped ahead of myself. The main reason I was back in England was to go to school.

Equipping me for life there was an epic that took Granny and Auntie Veronica many days of taking me around school outfitters to be measured and fitted. The list of clothing and accessories seemed endless. Winter uniform, summer uniform, overcoat, raincoat, two different dresses and a black veil for church with a bag to keep it in, cardigans, green woolly swimming costume, riding wear, summer hat (panama), winter hat (felt), (both with elastic stitched into them to keep them aboard), shoes, stockings, vests and knickers, suspender belts, gloves, Aertex shirts and baggy green knickerbockers for gym, blankets and eiderdowns, sheets and pillow cases, rubber hot water bottle, towels, face flannel, knives, forks, spoons, hockey stick and tennis racket.

As a boarder I had my first experience of being a number, in my case 35. This number had to be engraved onto each piece of cutlery, and poor Granny had to stitch a woven label into every item of clothing and bed linen. When the great heap of stuff was numbered and carefully folded, Granny packed it into a large trunk with a giant '35' stencilled on it, checking each item off against the printed list. How we got this thing to the railway station I don't remember. I know we didn't take a taxi, and we certainly didn't walk and couldn't have carried it to the bus stop. Anyway, somehow or other we got it on the train at Clapham Junction, a short ride to Waterloo Station. There, the trunk and I were loaded on to a second train, destination a little railway station in the stunningly beautiful Surrey countryside.

The convent school was perched upon a small green bump on the edge of the Surrey hills. Originally the 18$^h$ century building was a manor house, home to a succession of wealthy and notable persons before it became a convent. The L-shaped white two-storey building with its dark green shuttered windows was rather attractive, although the barred ground floor windows rang small alarm bells. Fifty acres of idyllic grounds included beautiful woods and spreading lawns, tennis courts, a swimming pool and a stable of horses and ponies. It wasn't the wild beauty and open spaces of Kenya, but it was a vast improvement on Clapham Junction, and I thought I could be very happy here.

At nine I was the youngest boarder by almost two years, as well as being one of only a handful of pupils who were not Roman Catholics. On my first day as I was lost, roaming around like the runt of a litter and trying to find out where I was meant to be, a larger girl with two ropey plaits swinging each side of her face came up to me. Without the slightest provocation she pushed me hard in the shoulder and said: "I'm Susan Jenkins and I'm the boss round here." Out of fear for what she might do next, and uncertain what response she expected of me, I launched myself at the plaits, swinging my whole weight on them while kicking her soundly around the shins. She ran away crying loudly and leaving thick strands of hair between my clenched fingers, and never bothered me again.

Being very small had its advantages, because the older girls 'adopted' me as a sort of overgrown doll, and took me under their collective wing, mothering me and spoiling me with sweets.

The nuns to whom my father had entrusted my physical and moral welfare and education at vast expense, were addressed as 'Mother.' Mother This, Mother That. It seemed an odd title for women who with rare exceptions displayed a maternal tenderness that would have frightened Mike Tyson.

Reverend Mother Superior was one exception. A tiny little prune as old as the hills, with a gentle, hypnotic voice and very dark, deep eyes in a face gouged with wrinkles, she was wise and understanding. Nobody was afraid of her although she was the supreme authority in our community. One other nun was universally popular: tall, freckled and red-eyebrowed she told terrifying ghost stories during evening meals. There was a whispered rumour that she was a reformed prostitute; precisely what that was we didn't know, but with that strange, inherent knowledge which little girls seem to have on such subjects, we had a sketchy idea. She was the person you could turn to with a problem, or when in need of comfort or sympathy, which was fairly regularly.

The school matron was a lay person with a glass eye. Once a week, she patrolled the dormitories with a large packet of thick pink and white sanitary towels tucked under her arm, shouting loudly "Hands up if you need bunnies' ears." This was no place for the prudish.

Dormitories were named after colours. Blue for younger girls, Green for middle schoolers and Pink reserved for the seniors. There was also eight-bed Orange dormitory, which seemed to serve as a kind of punishment block. When I first arrived I was in Blue, but not for long.

Orange dormitory was on the ground floor, somewhat isolated from the rest of the building, spooky and primitive with no running water nor, if I remember correctly, any heating. We used to get dressed under the bedclothes in winter. In the night, we could sometimes hear owls hooting, which one of the girls said were tramps calling to each other. The thought of ragged and possibly violent individuals surrounding us in the night on top of the ghost stories added to our fears.

It was terribly dark on winter nights, and the lavatory was a short distance from the dormitory. One bitter night rather than face the cold eerie trip, I wet the bed. In an effort to cover my tracks, so to speak, I loosened the plug of my hot water bottle (an item essential for survival in arctic Orange dormitory). When Mother Beastly came in the next morning to wake us up with the small jug of tepid water which served as our washing facility, I gave a little gasp of horror and cried "Oh no! My hot water-bottle has leaked all over the bed!" Mother Beastly was not deceived; maybe she'd seen the thing done before. Wrenching back the covers she exposed the white sheet which bore two individual stains, one of which was distinctly, unarguably yellow. All my companions in the dormitory came to have a look and a laugh. Funnily enough, I don't remember getting punished for that. Maybe laying in a cold wet bed most of the night was regarded as reasonable retribution.

Twice a week, we looked with trepidation at the bath schedule, posted to show who went where, and when. Reading the schedule was one of the low points of the week because we were all terrified of two of the bathrooms, Middle and End. They were set in a long, dark empty corridor on the first floor. From Middle, a window overlooked the grounds, but End just had a skylight, and there was a persistent tale that somebody had once hanged themselves in there. We went to these ghastly freezing places with our sponge bags and a towel and our hearts pounding madly from the fear of seeing ghosts. There were other more modern bathrooms, but during my years there I was only ever allocated to either End or Middle, to spend 15 minutes in tepid water and utter terror.

Hair-washing was once a week, after which we dried our heads with a towel. This was a two-person operation: somebody stood behind holding one end of the towel, whilst the dryee held the other end. We jerked the towel rhythmically backwards and forwards, faster and faster until we risked a broken neck by the force of the jerks. And it always made my frizzy hair stand up and out like a huge hairy halo.

Food was, like the curate's egg, good in parts, but only very small ones. Green pea soup was a thick sludge of deliciousness; 'dead babies' legs', a giant sausage roll served in slices, was pretty good, too. Often though it ranged from mediocre to disgusting: slimy spinach, grey boiled potatoes. The brown blancmange we called Thames Mud and tapioca, otherwise known as frog spawn, were not as unpleasant as they sound, but there were two horrors: jelly with rough scabs on its quivering surface, and the indescribably revolting warm watery custard flecked with lumps of brown, decaying banana with stringy bits in, whose vile taste was matched by its vomit-like texture. And you had to finish everything put in front of you. I soon learned to eat at normal speed, because the less you did to attract attention, the better.

Sometimes we didn't have enough to eat. Not often, but sometimes, when our complete evening meal was a one square inch cube of cheese and half an apple. It was insufficient for growing girls depleted by a full day of work and prayer. We left the dining room as hungry as when we entered it, with a thirteen-hour wait ahead before our next meal. I remember one night two of us cried with hunger and ate inches of toothpaste to try to pacify our hollow stomachs and rising nausea. That left an indelible memory of what the pains of hunger feel like, even when they are only a few hours old. It is not a small thing, as anybody who has suffered from it will testify. But it was a valuable experience and made a deep impression on me. While 'famine' and 'starvation' are just words, if you have ever been truly hungry it is something you never forget. It was our good fortune that Mother Red Eyebrows was on duty that evening. Hearing us talking late at night she came to ask why we were not sleeping. After she had listened, she went away and returned a few minutes later with a biscuit tin. In it were the stale crusts she saved to feed the birds, and that night she fed us apologetically, with the only thing she had to offer.

Usually our daily bread was far from fresh when it arrived in a van from town. During some sort of strike it came instead from nearby, fragrant, freshly-baked and still warm, stretchy and doughy. For about a week it was a pleasure to eat. We fervently hoped the strike would last forever, never mind if it crippled the country. But soon the dry, slightly grey slices embedded with small suspect lumps were back on the menu. In the dining room there was a large coal-burning stove which heated the room. I had an idea for how to improve the stale bread by toasting it on the hot surface. Mother Whoever noticed the slice laying on the hot plate. She strode across the room with a face like thunder and held the palm of my hand pressed on the stove for a few moments. She hoped, she said, that was a suitable warning against any repetition. I have to say it was pretty effective.

Punishment was generally administered swiftly – no hanging around wondering what would happen or when. Auntie Veronica sent me a watch for my birthday. I passed it to show a girl on another table in the dining room. With a single fluid swoop, Mother Thingy snatched it and thwacked it hard onto the edge of the table. The glass cracked and the hands stopped, and that was it, broken before I'd even put it on. Sooner or later I would have to explain its condition to Auntie Veronica. At that time no adult could or would believe that the nuns were anything other than saintly. Saying that they had burnt your hand or deliberately broken your watch would most likely result in a punishment for telling lies. Ironically, I had to invent a lie to explain the state of the watch. I think I said it was hit by a hockey stick during a match.

Sunday tea was a bizarre event. It was the one afternoon of the week when we had cake. During the rest of the week we went in an orderly manner into the dining room when the bell rang, and took our places on our benches, eight to a table. On Sundays, the exterior doors to the dining area were locked until one minute before 4.00pm. In the centre of each table on Sundays was a plate containing eight slices of cake. Seven of these slices were dry, crumbly fruitcake. One slice, however, was luscious, exquisitely gooey chocolate cake – two glossy brown layers of springy sponge stuck together by a generous layer of chocolate cream and crowned with chocolate icing. Outside the locked doors, a crowd of ravenous and determined girls waited, with our index fingers stuck in our mouths. The moment the doors were unlocked we stampeded down the corridor trampling beneath our little feet any who fell. Flying into the dining room to our table we stabbed a saliva-moistened finger into the chocolate cake. First finger in won. Nobody wanted cake with somebody else's spit in it. I'm proud to say that although the smallest member of our table, in fact the smallest girl in school, I got the chocolate cake more often than not.

*Was there some point to this competition?* I've often wondered. Perhaps it was just a harmless bit of fun watching a horde of girls flattening their friends in their determination to get a decent piece of cake. *Or was it a sweepstake?* Imagine each nun betting on the winning child at each table. The nun who selects the most wins is allowed to wear a pair of high heels for a day, or spend 15 minutes dancing to rock and roll. Can you see them lined up out of sight, watching the horde of chocolate-crazed kids, and shouting: "Come on you little beauty! Go on, kick her out of the way! That's it! Oh, you stupid fool of a child! Push! Kick! Use your elbows! Go on!" Can you see them jumping up and down, waving their arms, biting their knuckles as the contest was fought out? I can.

The kitchen was forbidden territory, but once I was sent there on an errand. On a large round tray was a heaped pyramid of Quality Street chocolates, and 24 tall glasses of what looked like Coca Cola, with a thick head of frothy cream (Stout, in fact). I ran back into the dining room shouting that we were going to have a surprise treat. Nobody believed me, which was just as well. A little later we glimpsed the tray and glasses heading into the refectory, which is where the 24 nuns ate.

At the beginning of each term pupils met and formed a group at Waterloo station. We'd all be in our smart uniforms, ready to catch the train to the station where we'd be greeted by the station mistress who had a port wine stain covering more than half her face. From there a coach delivered us to the school. On arrival the first thing we had to do was dutifully hand over our tuck boxes. Those were the rules.

Our term's supplies of treats had to be given to Mother Greedy, who would, she said, lock them carefully away and distribute them over the course of the term. My tuck box was packed by Auntie Veronica, and filled with fruit cake, chocolate bars, boiled sweets and a jar of a delicious malt, sticky gloop called Virol that was said to be good for growing children. Once the tuck boxes had been taken into Mother Greedy's custody, that was the last we ever saw of them or any of their contents. As if she had waved a magic wand over them, they disappeared without trace.

One term I managed to get the Virol out of the box before handing it in. It was a rich brown substance based on malt extract and similar in appearance to the viscous grease used by garage mechanics to lubricate engine parts, but it tasted divine. I took it and sat hidden among the coats and veil bags in the cloakroom, scooping it up with my fingers. It was a messy process, but rewarding for the first few minutes. Anybody who remembers Virol, though, will know that to sit and eat a whole jar in the space of about 20 minutes can only have one result, which leads to never again wanting to see or hear of Virol.

On Sunday evenings after the mad scramble for the piece of chocolate cake, Mother Greedy presided over 'Tuck shop.' There we could buy sweets to replace those she'd stolen. The selection was limited and not very exciting and seemed to be mainly those bitter little rubbery Pontefract cakes. I learned to hide some of my supplies in my clothing at the beginning of term. However they had to be consumed rapidly, because there were frequent impromptu raids into our drawers. If sweets were found, punishment would follow.

Juniors normally shuttled by coach to the junior school about a mile from the main building, except in wintry conditions when snow and ice coated the roads. On those days we walked in a nice orderly crocodile. Our days started early – they had to as there was so much to cram into them. At 6.30am a nun woke us up to wash, make our beds and be in chapel for Mass at 7.00am. After Mass was breakfast, preceded by grace, and followed by a brief prayer of thanksgiving. On arrival at junior school we celebrated morning prayers. At 10.30am, I think it was, a bell tolled and we stood for benediction; at mid-day we stood for the Angelus, and before and after lunch we said prayers. Something else took place at 4.00pm maybe it was another Angelus or benediction.

Then it was back to the main building to do our homework before assembling once more in the chapel for the evening service. Supper was sandwiched in between more prayers. Then it was time for bed, but not before we had knelt on the floor of the dormitory with a lighted candle in our hands, facing a Madonna who watched us sadly from one end of the room. It was a religious maniac's paradise.

One small, but enjoyable, thing during those final prayers at night, on our knees on the linoleum, was to allow molten candle wax to drip into the palm of my hand. Once I had amassed a sufficient quantity I would mould a tiny effigy of whichever nun I felt most deserving, and snap or twist off its head.

It was not that I didn't like chapel, it was simply that there was too much of it. It was like eating a whole jar of Virol every day. I begrudged having to get up at 6.30am on a bitter winter morning in

66

an unheated dormitory to attend Mass, especially as I was not a Catholic. There was one particular activity that I think we all dreaded: the Stations of the Cross. We knelt on the hard floor of the chapel holding a rosary at face level and saying the entire thing. It could be done in about 5 minutes if we were quick, but seemed eternal, and it had to be repeated before each of 14 plaques representing Christ's journey from the garden of Gethsemane to his crucifixion at Golgotha. If you want to experience agony, a good way to start is by kneeling on a hard wooden floor with both arms raised over your head for an hour. It was a torture worthy of Torquemada.

I would try almost anything to avoid Stations of the Cross, and if one of the holy Mothers felt I wasn't sufficiently devout, she would remind me that it was for the good of my eternal soul. I needed God's loving forgiveness more than most. Adultery was a sin. What a good thing they didn't know about my stealing years.

Sunday was a particularly busy day churchwise. For the evening service we changed into a dark green and slightly scratchy woollen dress with a detachable cream Peter Pan collar that was attached to the dress with press studs. And always, of course, anchored to our heads with lengths of elastic were the black nylon veils. For particularly holy days like Corpus Christi we wore special white satin dresses while we meandered around the grounds of the school, strewing rose petals romantically at various points along the way marked by religious icons in little shrines.

There were aspects of chapel that I loved. The fragrance of incense wafting from the censer swung by the priest, and the nuns singing in Latin, their sweet voices so at odds with their natures. Some of the phrases I can still hear: "*et antiquum documentum, veneremur cenerui*". "*Ave sanctissima! Ave purissima!* Sinless and beautiful Star of the Sea." The words and music sounded so beautiful as the incense swirled in intoxicating clouds around our heads.

Our winter uniform was a green gymslip, cream shirt, tie, green cardigan, thick brown stockings held up with an uncomfortable suspender belt and sturdy lace-up shoes. For going out we wore a heavy camel hair overcoat and a green felt hat. The school was divided into four houses, all named after saints, and our uniform ties in diagonal green stripes of varying widths indicated which house we belonged to. I was in Thomas Aquinas.

Each term the houses competed to see which could accumulate the most brownie points for good behaviour, academic, religious and sporting excellence. The reward to the winning house was something pretty spectacular, usually an outing to a show in London. Thomas Aquinas had quite a struggle as we seemed to have the largest number of dunces, fools, weaklings and rebels on our side, so it was seldom we managed to win. In fact, I think it only happened once. Our reward was to go to see the musical which was the great hit of the time, South Pacific. It seemed too good to be true, and so it turned out. Somebody did something wrong and at the last moment our trip was cancelled. The runners-up took our places, and Thomas Aquinas spent the evening in detention in the chemistry laboratory. Don't mess with the holy sisters – retribution was swift and merciless.

The school swimming pool was unheated and open-air. Swimming was obligatory all year round. Only two excuses were acceptable for not swimming: cold or period. Non-swimmers stood fully-clothed in a line beside the pool, and the lay games mistress barked at each in turn: "Cold or period?" requiring a loud answer to which everybody else was privy. Forget about chicken pox, flu, broken limbs or dysentery. If you didn't have either a cold or a period you put on your costume and jumped in. We spent many a foggy morning splashing about quite happily in the water which seemed warmer than the external temperature. One of our classmates was a girl four years older than the rest of us, and slightly slow mentally. She compensated by being excessively well developed physically. Our regulation swimming costumes were of green wool, decorously cut just below the neck at the front, with cross-over straps at the back. Judy, our classmate appeared one morning wearing her costume back to front. The cross-over straps lifted and separated distinctly from each other two gigantic mammaries mottled blue and purple by the cold. We who had not yet achieved such advanced development gawped in amazement as poor Judy blinked confusedly at the unusual attention she was attracting.

We were pretty normal little schoolgirls – happy, sad, playful, spiteful, and hopeful. We amused ourselves in our free time by gang wars, locking the enemy in the tennis courts or games lockers and holding secret meetings to plot our next campaign. One of us had read in a comic that you could cut out tiny paper silhouettes of skeletons and stick them to the front of a torch. Theoretically when the torch was switched on and pointed at a dark wall, a life-sized skeleton would appear. Although we spent long hours trying to cut miniature skeletons out of paper, that plan came to nothing.

Somehow we came by a large bottle of Milk of Magnesia, one of the popular laxatives at that time. Curious to see its effect, we decided to try it out on some other children during break-time, the mid-morning period when we drunk our obligatory milk and ate 'dead fly biscuits.' Unanimously elected as Doctor, I personally administered very generous doses to four of our classmates. They were subsequently confined to the infirmary for the next two days and I was in a lot of trouble. I had no intention or desire to make them ill. We simply wanted to know what Milk of Magnesia did.

It was best not to be ill. If you had to go to the Infirmary under the auspices of Mother Merciless, you'd damned well wish you hadn't. She was a large woman with a deeply purple face, wide down-turned mouth and heavy eyebrows beneath the white wimple that dug deeply and fascinatingly into her brow. She could tell from fifty yards that there was nothing at all wrong with you. I had a festering abscess under a tooth for over a week, and sobbed through the night from the pain and grizzled through the day, but Mother Merciless said I didn't have toothache, and that was it. I had to wait until Nan came to take me out for the day and took me to a dentist for treatment. And later I wished she hadn't complained to Reverend Mother about Mother Merciless, who dosed me with syrup of figs as a lesson, ramming it painfully into my mouth with a large sharp spoon. It causes a similar reaction to Milk of Magnesia. After that, I learned not to bother Mother Merciless.

In 1957, a major flu pandemic struck the planet. It was known as Asian flu, and claimed approximately nine million lives worldwide.

It managed to find its way to the convent. Girls started going down like skittles. Nobody died, but many were really rather ill. The victims were immediately confined to the Infirmary under the mean eye of Mother Merciless. I developed a dry cough and a very sore throat that I did my best to disguise so as not to incur her wrath. But every so often I was taken with an irrepressible fit of coughing. "Stop that, Susan!" she would roar. "If you're going to get it, you will, you don't have to pretend. We're far too busy looking after girls who really *are* sick."

I think she regarded it as a personal defeat when I finally collapsed and joined the other girls in the sick bay, where we were quarantined for three weeks to avoid spreading the virus. This was a most fortunate event because it coincided with the start of our school holidays. Instead of staying with long-suffering Granny and her sour little spouse, I spent several very pleasant weeks with a group of friends. Once the initial symptoms had passed we had nothing to do but enjoy ourselves within the confines of the sick bay. One of the girls came from a wealthy local family, and her mother arrived daily with hampers crammed with treats and delicacies to be shared amongst us. It's the best illness I ever had.

I must have been feeling sorry for myself one evening, and told the girls in the dormitory that I'd swallowed a bottle of aspirin. One of them ran to get Mother Merciless, who acted swiftly. She half-filled a tumbler with coarse salt, the remaining half with water, and she tilted my head back and poured the mixture down my throat. I retched and vomited violently for a seeming eternity, until she was satisfied that I was completely empty, and had learned a well-deserved lesson. She didn't ask why I had pretended I was committing suicide. For years afterwards, the slightest smell of salt made me heave.

# Chapter Eight

# Holidays

My best friend was a daygirl called Fenella. She was Scottish, a Roman Catholic with flame-red curly hair and very pale skin. There were certain things she could do as a Catholic that I was unable to participate in. I wanted to share with her taking Holy Communion and making confession, so in one of my weekly letters to my father I said I wanted to become a Catholic. His reaction was one of horror. He proposed that I should wait until I was a little older before committing myself.

Fenella had an older brother who shared her Celtic colouring. I was often invited to go home with her for weekends. Her family were extremely kind and hospitable, but they mostly walked around with no clothes on. In their household it was perfectly normal for two adults and a 19-year old boy to wander round the house and garden and eat at table stark naked in front of a ten or eleven-year-old schoolgirl guest.

Our little gang cultivated a deep interest in understanding fully what we called the FOL, an acronym we were certain nobody else would recognize. Fenella had a head start coming from a family with no inhibitions about displaying their anatomy. This was a complicated situation. Although we were the closest of friends, neither was prepared to be outdone by the other. Consequently we both maintained that we were fully aware of the process of human reproduction. At the same time we used every possible means to extract further information from each other without appearing to be lacking in knowledge. It would go something like:

"Of course, I suppose you know how... ?"

"Of *course* I do!"

"Well, go on then, prove it. Tell me what you know."

"Why should I? If you already know, why are you asking me?"

"I'm only making sure *you* really know, and aren't just *saying* you do."

Then a bell would probably sound and it would be time for prayers or lessons and a respite from our skirmishes.

As the end of the summer term approached, Fenella said she was going to ask her brother whether he had done it, gone all the way. If so, she'd get him to tell her in graphic detail and simple words what it was like and how it was correctly done. She was confident that Alexander would be perfectly willing to share his experiences with her. In turn she would share with us the full, unabridged, unexpurgated and explicit details.

Academically I didn't shine, except at English and French. To my eternal regret I had opted out of Latin, as one of my friends had said scornfully that it was 'a dead language'. I didn't know what a dead language was, but it didn't sound like much fun.

At speech day I was to receive a prize for French. In honour of such a rare event Granny and Auntie Veronica travelled to the school to sit and watch the ceremony and applaud this momentous occasion when I'd achieved something positive. The prize was a book called *Delorme in Deep Water* and my name and achievement were written in splendid Copperplate and stuck inside the book's hard cover. Although I was proud of it, for some reason I never read it. After the presentation, Granny and Auntie Veronica met Fenella's parents and talked for a long time. Before we all went our separate ways for the long summer holidays I reminded her not to forget her vital mission. Confidently she assured me when we met again on the first day of the next term, she would be in full possession of all the necessary facts.

Being at boarding school I didn't know any local children in Clapham Junction, so I spent much of my time amusing myself. I read voraciously, making daily trips to the public library, and when the opportunity arose, pulled out the scandalous News of the World from where Granddad sneakily hid it under the cushion on his seat. I must have read just about every book in the library, and when I'd run out of reading material, I designed a mini-hoopla game. Collecting as many small items as I could rake together, I lined them up on the front room floor and spent endless hours trying to toss plastic bracelets over them. When I'd 'won' them all, I started the process over again.

Unless Auntie Veronica took Jennifer and myself to a museum, there wasn't anything else to pass the time except sporadic shopping trips with Granny 'down the junction'. Long walks down the length of Lavender Hill to Clapham Junction where we window-shopped, shopped for fish, for meat, for vegetables. Once fully laden we hauled slowly back up the hill weighed down with brown carrier bags with string handles. Every so often our journey was punctuated by protracted conversations with other old ladies.

Only once did I decline to go with Granny on one of her trips, but the little bastard in the chair beside the fire snarled:

"Go on, get out and use your bloody legs. That's what God gave them to you for."

So I went.

Nan always came to take me out at the weekends, but the holidays in Clapham seemed long, and I couldn't wait to get back to school. Traditionally Granny took me to Battersea Fun Fair during the last week of the summer holidays. Originally known as the Festival Pleasure Gardens they were a wonderful place of penny slot machines, dodgem cars, hair-raising rides like the Big Dipper and motorcycles that raced each other up and round the vertical Wall of Death. The gentler ride called The Caterpillar was my choice – wooden carriages circling round and round, up and down and a green canvas hood coming up and over us. That was as much excitement as I wanted. I could have a toffee apple, ice cream or candy floss while we watched the extraordinary clock that did unpredictable things each quarter hour, with mechanical people and animals popping out of it from different places. Then we would go and pet the animals in the small children's zoo where a goat once ate all the buttons off the smart new cardigan that Granny had only just finished knitting for me. And always on the last day of the school holiday she cooked my favourite meal. She was the undisputed champion of suet pudding makers, cooking them in the time-honoured way – shaped into a roll, tied in a piece of muslin and steamed for a couple of hours. The interior was light and fluffy and the outside a shiny, white smooth film. I ate half with ham and an onion sauce as a first course, and the remainder as dessert with golden syrup. If I close my eyes I can smell, see and taste them now. What a voluptuous thing was Granny's suet pudding.

# Chapter Nine

## Homesick

Because Fenella was a daygirl and delivered directly to the junior school by her parents, we didn't meet on the first day of the new term until break-time, just after the 10.30am prayer ritual. During morning classes she passed me a note.

It said: 'I've got something really important to tell you'.

*How could time pass so slowly?* When the bell went we fled to the playground to collect our compulsory bottles of milk. I said, "Come on, tell me!"

"No, wait, let's go somewhere private."

We huddled behind a tree, and after peering around her to make sure we were alone, and rolling her eyes dramatically, she said:

"Your Granny didn't want you, but your Auntie wouldn't have you."

I stared at her in amazement.

"How do you know?"

"I heard them talking about you at prize giving. Your Auntie said she'd had enough with your cousin; she said she was a bloody liability. Your Dad asked her to have you too, but she said one was more than enough. So your Granny has to put up with you. She hopes you'll go back to Africa soon."

"Yes, but what did Alexander say about, you know?"

"Oh, he was in Scotland for the holidays and I didn't get a chance to ask him. But what do you think about your Granny not wanting you?"

"I don't care," I shrugged.

But I did. Of course I did. *What child wants to be told it's unwanted?*

Fenella's failure to complete her mission initially took my mind off what she had said. It wasn't until after lights out in the dormitory that night that the impact of her words hit home and I cried for the first time I could remember. Mummy had gone away. My father had sent me away. Granny didn't want me. Auntie Veronica wouldn't have me. Fenella's words crystallised everything that had happened over the last four years, and my heart ached to be back in Africa.

Over and over again on the record player in the gym I played *West of Zanzibar* and Tommy Steele singing his latest hit, *Nairobi*. Never mind that there were no cockatoos, sand dunes and flying fishies, bing bongs and bom-a-tom-toms, Nairobi was my home. The tunes went around and around in my head and most nights I rocked myself to sleep to their words.

*Without Nan, what would I have done?*

My other special friend Victoria came from a family who owned a flower farm at Bognor. Often I went there for the holidays. With acres to run riot in and the freedom to do as we liked, these were happy times, although for somebody afflicted with hay fever a flower farm isn't perhaps the most suitable place to stay at the height of summer. I either sneezed day and night or spent much of the time dozing from the effect of anti-histamines. Staying with friends in their homes I forgot my loneliness and how much I missed my father, Pluto and Minetta. And of course Mummy. *Where was she now? When would the long time be over so I could see her again?*

I was always embarrassingly aware that I couldn't reciprocate invitations. Clapham Junction might have been the largest and busiest railway junction in the country, where the Waterloo and Victoria lines united and crossed, and a seventh heaven for train-spotters; but with Granny farting and Granddad grunting from his chair, it didn't have a lot to offer my schoolfriends.

Sundays at the convent were generally good days, once the protracted Mass was over and providing there was no particularly holy event to celebrate. There was no homework, we were free to do much as we wanted and dress in 'mufti' – our own clothes. One of our little band's favourite pastimes was to walk about in the woods reading the gravestones of the dogs that lay buried there, reminders that once this place had been a private home: 'Captain, faithful hound, 1923 – 1933' 'Bouncer, 1928 – 1940'. We would kneel before these slabs and work ourselves into tears, and huddle in little groups sharing our grief. It was tremendous fun.

Each week we were given a certain amount of pocket money. Apart from the sweets we bought to replace our stolen tuck, the only other thing we could use this money for was buying holy pictures. Of varying sizes these were rather attractive. Some had golden borders and each portrayed either Christ, the Virgin Mary or a saint. They bore quotations from the Bible, and meaningful words. We collected them and exchanged them with each other. As pretty as my collection was, it could not satisfy the gap within me that could only be filled by having a pet. I yearned for something to cuddle. There were two dogs living at the school, Punch, a black Labrador, and Judy a greyhound, but sharing them with hordes of other girls wasn't at all satisfactory. I wanted a pet that was uniquely mine.

One of my friends, a day girl, said she could get me a mouse. I handed over a fistful of pocket money saved by not buying holy pictures for a few weeks, and she smuggled into school a beautiful little champagne-coloured mouse with pink eyes and nose and twitchy whiskers. I couldn't afford a cage for it so it lived partly in my drawer with my jumpers and sometimes in the bag with my veil. But most of the short time it was with me, my mouse lived inside my pocket. I fed it on biscuit crumbs and morsels saved from meals, and loved it to bits. Then one of the Mothers discovered it and threw it out of the window.

On Sunday afternoons a Mother, usually popular Mother Red Eyebrows, took us for long walks through the green, hilly countryside. Very often we would find ourselves scrambling up Box Hill. It was a hard struggle but worth it for the spectacular views from the 700 ft. summit, and the rapid slithery descent. It was on these walks that one of the older girls taught us to belch at will. It's quite easy once you have the hang of it. Farting was another matter, some could (they could even play rudimentary tunes), and some couldn't. I fell into the latter category, and missed out on a display given by the girl who had bought the mouse for me. The daughter of a local publican and more earthy than some of the delicately raised girls, she demonstrated how to set on fire your personal gas production. Only self-starting farters were admitted to the demonstration, but a friend who was there assured me it was rather spectacular.

Our walks generally lasted about two hours and got us back to school just in time for the chocolate-cake contest.

I was not an angel but my misdemeanours were innocent. One day we planned a dance of the seven veils and smuggled our black veils from their neat little bags in the cloakroom into our dormitory. We waited for a while until after lights-out and turned them back on again. Then with much giggling we took it in turns to drape ourselves in the black nylon squares and gyrate around the room weaving our arms as sinuously as 11-year-olds are able to. Until this episode we hadn't realised that our dormitory was overlooked from the second floor at right angles by one of the nun's rooms. The light attracted her attention and swift wrath. There would be no horse-riding for anybody at the weekend, and no tuck shop for us either. The latter wasn't much of a problem. We gave our money to friends who bought on our behalf. This required some ingenuity because Mother Greedy watched what everybody bought like a hawk. If you spent more than your weekly allowance she wanted to know the hows and whys.

The escapade that earned me the most Draconian punishment as far as I remember was designing a slide during a hot summer. With the help of the other girls in the dormitory, I manoeuvred my bed out of the window, so that one end rested on the lawn and the high end was supported by its legs hooked over the window frame. We had tremendous fun while it lasted, which wasn't long at all. It was probably the noise we made as we tumbled in turns down the mattress onto the cool soft grass. All too soon a heavenly Mother erupted through the door, and she was not amused. My accomplices scrambled back into their beds and feigned sleep, but it was difficult to plead my innocence with my bed still out of the window. While the rest of the dormitory snored unconvincingly, I struggled to get the bed back inside, which proved far more difficult than getting it out in the first place, especially as now I was single-handed, Mother not being prepared to help. But once it was back where it belonged, she curtly told me to follow her. No, leave my slippers and dressing gown, come just as I was – in a pair of cotton pyjamas. I stood all through the night on the clammy green linoleum, in the dark, in the long corridor that led to the dining rooms. I was cold, frightened out of my wits and feeling extremely sorry for myself. At daylight the nuns started going about their holy business, bustling around and ignoring me. I might as well have been invisible.

Somebody had been drawing figures in the grime on the windows of the gym. *Why were the windows so dirty? Shouldn't one of the Mothers have kept the place clean?* Mother Miserable wanted to know who had done it, or there would be no tuck shop. Nobody owned up. As I was regularly in trouble, either for things I had done, or had not done, I decided to play the heroine. That way everybody could get their supply of sweets and of course a friend would get mine for me, so there was nothing to lose. I confessed to Mother Miserable who sent me to Reverend Mother Superior, the kindly withered old lady who was so out of place amongst the thugs around her.

"Now, Susan, what have you been up to this time?"

"I drew the pictures on the windows, Reverend Mother."

"Did you, dear? And what were the pictures you drew?"

I hadn't the faintest idea, not having seen them.

"Oh Susan, you're in trouble often enough, you don't need to own up to things you haven't done. Now run along."

Tuck shop opened that Sunday.

My only wicked act was, in a fit of extreme boredom during an eternal church service, mindlessly carving my initials in one of the elegant pews of the chapel. It was not intended as a deliberate or evil act of vandalism. I didn't really know why I was doing it. Sorrowfully Reverend Mother said that I had done something very wrong, and I would have to be expelled. I spent the day thinking how much I would miss my friends and the ponies, but hoping that I'd be sent back to Africa.

Later that day Reverend Mother administered her gentle mercy again. If I was truly sorry for what I had done, I could stay. I think my father had to pay for repairs, but I wasn't sent packing in disgrace.

# Chapter Ten

# Darned Darning

There was a particular magazine, something about missionaries, that lay about in the classroom. In it we found an advertisement saying: 'Buy a black baby for 2/6d' (12½p/20cents in current money). We interpreted this literally. A group of us decided to pool our resources and send away for one of the exquisite chubby little black babies pictured on the advertisement. It wasn't a lot of money; we could save sufficient between us in about four weeks. We started drawing up complicated schedules as to who would look after the baby when. It would be a problem during lessons, especially if it cried, and we were fairly sure that if one of the Mothers discovered it, it would follow my mouse out of the window. After some debate we decided to confide in Mother Red Eyebrows. She could be counted on as a staunch ally and would never betray a secret. She listened patiently to our plan, and agreed that the little black baby we had chosen was quite bewitching, and that 2/6d was a modest price for such a fine infant. She asked what we planned to do with it during the school holidays. Were we sure our parents/grandparents would be happy to have an unexpected baby in the family? And what would we do when it started growing up walking, talking and needing to go to school?

We really hadn't considered any of these eventualities. After talking through the project we agreed that it was going to be far too demanding. Our lifestyle was not suited to welcome the little black stranger, so we bought extra sweets instead.

The highlight of my week was the Saturday horse ride through woods and fields, over hills and through valleys and bracken paths, and sometimes through the beautiful grounds of nearby Polesden

Lacey. There were some fine horses in the stables, Polly a dark brown cob, Uncle James a huge Shire and my favourite, a dapple-grey pony called Grey Lady. The stables were run independently of the school and beyond the malevolent influence of the nuns. Once on a horse nothing mattered, even if it was winter and frizzling frost burnt my nose and fingers, or high summer and my eyes and nose streamed from hay fever, this was a couple of hours in paradise.

A cloud hovered menacingly on the horizon – darning. On Saturday mornings one-eyed matron walked into the dining room during breakfast with a clipboard. On the clipboard was a list of numbers, and if your number was called you would spend the morning darning. That would probably mean missing the 10.00am ride. Rides weren't interchangeable: if you missed it, you missed it. I used to sit with a lump in my throat and fear in my heart when I was booked to ride at 10.00am. Matron slowly read out the numbers of those girls detained for darning: "101, 16, 39," long hesitation, "66 and," with a sad little smile in my direction, "oh dear, 35 again! Really, dear, I just don't know *what* you *do* with your stockings." I used to check my stockings minutely each week when they went to laundry and they never had holes in them on the outbound journey. But as sure as Matron had a glass eye, they always returned with ladders.

Under Matron's single watchful eye we darned in one of the classrooms while she sat knitting. I worked feverishly with short, knotty lengths of brown wool trying to fill the holes in the bloody stockings, watching the clock in a race to get to the stables before the 10.00am ride left. I forgot to mention that apart from being half-blind, Matron was almost deaf. She generally used a hearing aid but during darning duty she sat in a quiet, knitting world of her own. One morning the ceiling fell down on me as I stitched madly. A slight trickle of dust, a crack and rumble and the ceiling settled onto my head and shoulders in a soft, fragrant, dusty white pile. There was no weight in it, so while the rest of the darning detail tittered with delight, trying not to giggle (Matron didn't like girls giggling) I walked to where she sat in her silent, semi-sighted world and waited for her to notice me. After a few minutes she looked up, startled and asked what on earth I had been doing.

"The ceiling has fallen in," I said dramatically.

"What?"

I bellowed towards her ear: "The ceiling. The ceiling has fallen down."

"Don't be so ridiculous. Tell me what you've done. You bad girl."

The rest of the class sat laughing, pointing at the ragged gap where that part of the ceiling which I was now wearing had previously lived.

A maintenance man arrived and found that the space above had been used for storing apples in the days when the building was still a private house. Over the years the fruit had gone about its business of slowly rotting into a putrefying soup that had dissolved the plaster ceiling.

On a good day I could stitch the stocking ladders sufficiently well to satisfy Matron's poor eyesight. Then I'd rush to change into riding clothes and get to the stables in time for the morning ride. If Matron wasn't happy, the brown wool had to be dug out of the stockings, leaving an even larger hole to be repaired, and the tiresome process started again. That definitely meant I wouldn't be riding that weekend.

One day the lady who ran the stables asked why I was so often late, when she knew I was about the most enthusiastic and pony-mad child in the school. I explained about the darning. After that, bless her, my name invariably appeared on the list for the afternoon ride, a major victory over Matron.

By now I had been dividing my time between the dual delights of the convent and Clapham Junction for three and a half years. Although given the choice I wouldn't want to do it again, it hadn't been all that bad. Despite the sly cruelty of the nuns and the demands of prayer, life at the convent had been mostly enjoyable.

I had heard nothing of my mother since she left Kenya with her future husband, apart from a Christmas present of the book *Lorna Doone* that Nan gave me, saying Mummy had sent it. I still have it.

On one of my regular visits to spend the weekend with Nan, she sat me down to write 'thank you' letters to all the sweet old ladies, her friends, who used to give me little presents and biscuit-and-tea-flavoured kisses on my cheeks. Nan had to go out for a while, but left me with her red leather zip-up writing case and a list of names to write to. Once I'd finished the letters and she still wasn't back I investigated the contents of the case. I found some newspaper cuttings tucked into one pocket. They were reports of attempts that Mummy had made to write to me at school, letters that had been returned unopened. She had come to the school and been refused permission to see me by the nuns acting, they said, on my father's instructions. Mummy had been to court to appeal against an order made by my father, but had lost her case. She was not allowed any contact with me.

I didn't mention to Nan that I had seen these cuttings, and she didn't mention it either. But I had understood the message. Mummy had not forgotten me. More than twenty years later I would suddenly feel the most terrible anger towards my father for preventing my mother from seeing me.

During the holidays, one day Granny said: "I've got something to tell you. You're going back to Africa."

This was the news I had longed for ever since the foggy evening almost four years previously when I'd arrived with Flicker in wintry London. I was going back home to the sunshine and smiling black people, to Daddy and his dog Pluto, and my cat Minetta.

"Your father has married again," she continued, producing from a drawer a glossy black and white photograph. There was Daddy looking very handsome in a dinner jacket, seated at a table with a group of smiling people.

She handed me the photograph. I looked at the vivacious blonde laughing up at my father and said, "She looks like a really nice lady."

Granny said very gently, "It's not her, it's the other one." She pointed to a beaky nosed woman with wispy grey hair and hard, cold eyes. She was the only person in the photograph not smiling.

"As a matter of fact," continued Granny, "he's been married for quite a long while, and you've got a little sister who is almost a year old."

84

It was rather a lot to take in. I wondered why Daddy hadn't mentioned any of this in his letters to me.

After one more term at boarding school, I was going back home to Africa, where I belonged.

For the end of term we were putting on a production of a play called *Daddy Longlegs*. For the first time I had secured a minor role and was very excited to be making my acting debut. We rehearsed on the stage in the gym over and over again until everybody was word perfect. Our excitement level was off the scale. Then two things happened. Firstly, Mother Somebody caught me talking when I shouldn't have been. She pushed me off the stage, a drop to the floor of about three feet, and replaced me with an understudy.

Although the Mother hadn't physically injured me apart from a couple of grazes, the expulsion was a mortal blow. I hurt for the rest of the day, but worse was to come.

On the final day of term and my very last day at the school, as parents were arriving for prize-giving and the play in which I no longer had a part, a loud announcement called for everybody to assemble immediately in the gym. One of the nuns came onto the stage and without any noticeable emotion broke the news. On the way back from the junior school prize-giving (I'd moved up the main school the previous year), the car carrying Reverend Mother Superior and two other nuns had been involved in an accident at the bottom of the gloomy rhododendron-lined road leading to the school. Reverend Mother had been killed instantly.

Together with shock and sorrow, I felt a raging anger. *Why her? Why the gentle little lady who wouldn't harm a soul? Why not one of the others, one of the mean, spiteful ones?*

We were told it was a blessing for Reverend Mother to have been taken to God's merciful bosom, but I resented God very much. Not just for what he had done to Reverend Mother, but for all the things he'd done to me. I began to question why somebody supposedly all powerful allowed so much unhappiness in the world. If he was omnipotent, why didn't he stop bad things happening? If he was able to do anything, and allowed terrible things to happen, then how could he be merciful?

The play and speeches were cancelled. I said goodbye to all my friends. We promised to write to each other, but we never did. With a mixture of emotions I left the convent for good.

# Chapter Eleven

# Homeward Bound

On the morning of the day when my father was coming to joyfully reclaim me, Granny paid particular attention to my violent hair, which seemed to grow thicker and curlier by the day. Cutting it was more a job for a topiarist than a hairdresser. My frantic efforts to flatten and straighten it were a waste of time. It seemed to gain some sort of satanic energy from anything it touched. Granny on the other hand thought my hair was wonderful. She brushed gooey stuff from a tube onto it to make it gleam.

The tube of gooey stuff lived with the toothpaste and the Glymiel Jelly for her hands in a drawer in the dresser where Joey's cage stood. As she rubbed and brushed the tube's contents thoroughly through my hair, I smelled mint. We both realised too late that something was wrong. My wild hair was matted with slightly gritty toothpaste.

There was a last minute panic and re-wash of the hair. That entailed boiling several kettles of water, and the lathery toothpaste was difficult to remove. A vigorous towelling dry created an unfortunate giant frizzy nimbus radiating around my head. No amount of mashing with hands or damping could control it. Granny moaned distractedly as she tried to make me look less like an electrified Hottentot. Her panic was infectious. If I looked so awful, perhaps my father wouldn't want me.

"Try to look nice, like a good girl," said Granny. I stood in a pink dress, waiting for the moment when Daddy would come and pick me up and hug me. He'd tell me how I'd grown and how pleased he was to see me, as of course he would be after all this time. I tried to look as beguiling as I possibly could, notwithstanding the damp fuzzy hair that still smelt lingeringly of toothpaste.

From the street came the noise of the knocking of a taxi engine, the heavy clunking of its doors, footsteps on the stone path, and the front door opening. After a few moments of silence, low voices murmured and then the footsteps began again, slowly, squeakily, on the linoleum of the long corridor leading to the front room.

Granny stood holding my hand firmly, as if I might turn and run, but I was rooted to the spot and holding my breath. Through the two frosted glass panels I saw shadowy movement. The round door knob turned. There was my father, tall, blond, handsome, just as I remembered him.

Instead of coming straight into the room, he held the door and ushered in another person who was clutching a carrycot awkwardly to her side.

In my euphoria at going back to my home, in truth I hadn't given very much thought to the new mother and sister. Now here they were. When I had pictured being reunited with Daddy, I'd thought it would be just the two of us.

I started to step towards my father. I had imagined a crushing embrace, being lifted off my feet and swung around. Quite why, I don't know, as I can't remember he had ever lifted me off the ground or swung me in the air before. Somehow it's what I'd expected he would do after nearly four years without seeing me.

"Hello, Sue," he said, putting his arm around the grey-eyed, grey-haired woman and forestalling my movement. "This is Helen, and this is your new little sister."

He ushered me towards them, and I peered into the carrycot and tried to think of something to say.

I was still waiting for the hug.

"I expect you remember Helen. She nursed you when you were in hospital."

"Hello," I said, looking into her face. I didn't remember her. Grey spectral eyes stared back, coldly, silently.

*Where was the hug, the laugh, the delight at seeing me?*

Granddad, in the chair beside the fireplace, had not participated in any way, acknowledging my father's "Hello Dad," with his normal charismatic grunt, and returning to his scouring of the racing fixtures in the newspaper. Granny suggested putting the kettle on, but the taxi was waiting outside in the street with its noisy engine. My father and Helen hadn't even sat down. Helen hadn't spoken a word. We said quick goodbyes and Granny followed us to the front door. She kissed me and told me to try and be a good girl. Then we climbed into the taxi that took us to the docks for the voyage back to Kenya. We hardly talked – nobody seemed to know what to say. I felt more like an obligation rather than the centre of attention I had expected to be.

Looking back to that day, I suppose that they must have visited Granny earlier, while I was still at school. But at the time I was bewildered by the briefness of their visit and the fact that nobody asked after anybody.

It was September 1958 when we boarded the *Warwick Castle*, a sister ship to the *S.S. Kenya Castle* in the familiar lavender livery and red funnel. The noble lady had in an earlier life served as an aircraft carrier during the war, before being converted back to a passenger ship. Ecstatically I ran from deck to deck, explored the shops, the dining room, the swimming pool and library, all very much as I remembered. I galloped back to the cabin. Would we stop in Gibraltar again to see the apes? And there was a bigger swimming pool on this ship. Wouldn't it be wonderful to see the camels on the Suez Canal again! I wondered if the gully gully man would come and do more tricks with the baby chicks.

Nobody shared my enthusiasm, which was met with a deafening silence. My father steered me from the cabin into the passageway outside.

"Look, Sue. You mustn't keep talking about the last time we were on the ship. Remember, Helen wasn't with us then. You don't want to upset her, do you?"

"Why will she be upset?" I asked.

"Because last time there was someone else with us. Now Helen is here, and we don't want to make her feel uncomfortable. So stop talking about 'the last time.' There's a good girl."

I mustn't remember a previous happy time, because that would upset Helen.

Constantly anxious not to say the wrong thing, I became very cautious, thinking carefully before I spoke in case it upset Helen. Soon I hardly spoke at all. The ice creams still came around every morning, there was still tea on deck and in the library at 4.00pm, and deck-quoits and all those familiar things. The scenery was still as exotic, the ship as exciting, the weather as balmy. King Neptune came aboard as we crossed the Equator for the traditional dunking into a great vat of porridge. There were games and films, but it felt as if a permanent vague shadow hovered over us. We all shared a cabin. My father seemed rather quiet, wearing a permanent small smile on his face as if to reassure himself and everybody else that we were a nice happy little family.

The baby was fractious and Helen worried constantly about disease, insects, heat, germs and infections. When we were together there was virtually no conversation. I longed to be in Lower Kabete Road, in the familiar bungalow, in the privacy of my own room, with my cat. Sometimes, I briefly thought I'd even rather be back in Granny's house on Lavender Hill. But once we were back in Nairobi I knew everything would be all right.

In the meantime there was a horse aboard, a fine stallion going to South Africa. He lived in a stable on the crew deck below, and I watched him from behind a rail on the deck above. One of the sailors befriended and flirted with me; he made me laugh, and I spent most of every day hanging over the rail watching the horse and chatting with him. When we docked at Kilindini he handed me a little note with his address on it, and a box of Meltis Newberry Fruits. Unfortunately they are my least favourite sweets after Pontefract cakes, but I kept them as a souvenir until they were overrun with ants. *Are you still out there somewhere, Mick Fahey?*

# Chapter Twelve

## Changing Schools

The house looked the same, but it was not.

There were no African servants; the clock on the mantelpiece had vanished; there was no sign of Pluto, and I couldn't find Minetta. While my father and Helen were unpacking and dealing with the baby, I wandered around calling for her. She wasn't anywhere in the house, and she wasn't in the garden.

"Daddy. I can't find Minetta!"

My father explained that Minetta had been dirty in the house. She could have given us disease and illness, so it had been best for her to be put to sleep. It was very peaceful, and she hadn't felt any pain.

Unlike poor Minetta, I felt pain, a physical breaking of my heart. All the waiting to hold her again, to feel her sharp little claws kneading my shoulder, to hear her throaty purr. All the waiting for nothing. I didn't ask about Pluto because I didn't want to know what his fate had been.

At home life was peaceful if subdued. We no longer socialised with our old friends, the same people as when Mummy was here. Now there were new friends, a handful of Helen's nursing colleagues and their husbands.

If only at this time we had sat down together and discussed our new relationship, things might have turned out differently. My father never mentioned his marriage to Helen, nor ever suggested that I should regard her as a substitute for my mother. She did not tell me that she was glad to be part of our family, that she would enjoy looking after me, that she hoped we would be good friends. I think if we had had a chance to talk about our feelings we could have made things work out. But we didn't. Nothing was said.

When the new school term started I was back at Loreto Convent as a day girl. Church wasn't obligatory for the non-Catholics. This was a blessed relief as I felt I had already crammed as much prayer into my life in the last three and a half years as one person could possibly need.

Loreto Convent was a friendly, relaxed school and the daily journey there and back was happy, because that's the time I spent alone with my father. When we left the house in the morning, Helen watched in the driveway as we climbed into the car like a pair of polite strangers. Once we were out of sight he relaxed a little and for the short time we were together in the car we could be like a normal father and daughter. When it was just the two of us he became jovial and fun. After school I'd wait for him to collect me, watching the steps that led from the car park. He'd stand there looking like a film star, raising a hand to wave when he saw me. Happy times.

The syllabus here was quite different from that at the convent in Surrey. I was adrift in history and geography, hadn't done any physics or chemistry and was very behind in maths. Despite the considerable musical talent on my mother's side of the family I was hopeless at music and singing. I couldn't learn how to read music and I couldn't sing a note in tune. Our music teacher was very kind. "You can just sit and listen," she said, after my best renditions of *Lavender's blue, dilly dilly*, and *Rosy apples on the tree*. At the end of lessons she'd oblige us by singing some of the latest top ten hits. Only English and French and my accuracy as the netball team shooter redeemed me from being a total failure.

Life at Loreto was almost a pleasure, marred only by one particular nun. She and I did not like each other and she expressed her dislike physically – jabbing her fingers hard into the fastening of my bra until the hooks stuck into my skin, or by making me stand in front of the class and bray like a donkey. Neither of these techniques led to a better understanding of the subject she taught, mathematics. She also reminded me more than once that divorce was a sin against God, and would be punished on the Day of Reckoning. What was more, in the eyes of God, people who had been divorced were not married to their current partners, but living in a state of sin. As if I was responsible. As if it made any difference to me.

As an accountant my father was frustrated by my consistently poor maths marks, and unable to understand why I did so badly. The fact that I excelled in English and French did nothing to mitigate my poor performance in almost all other subjects. The syllabus had no similarity at all to that at my previous school and I was years behind most of my classmates in all subjects. One evening as I stared uncomprehendingly at my maths homework, he came into the room and looked over my shoulder.

"Why have you ripped the pages in your book?" he asked impatiently, picking up a shredded maths exercise book.

I explained that unless you got all your sums right, the nasty nun took a red ball-pen and pushed it hard into the bottom left-hand corner of the page, until it made a ragged hole. Then she ripped it with panache diagonally upwards, destroying the page and leaving a red slash on the page beneath. I told him about the bra fastening punishment, and the donkey and dog noises too. He wrote angrily to the school that evening, telling them I would not be returning to their chilly bosom the following term. That was the end of my convent schooling.

At Delamere Girls High School our gym skirts did not have to touch the ground when we knelt, as they had at the convents. Knees were not wicked. Also there was no distinction between girls of one religion and another. Buddhists, Muslims, Hindus and Christians were all treated equally.

There was no psychological or physical mistreatment here. Some of the teachers were strict, but they didn't instil fear. The worst that could happen to really bad girls was to have their name called at morning assembly. They'd then have to climb onto the stage and stand there in shame. I never had to do that. If you fell foul of a monitor they made you lie on the floor of the gym during the lunch break and count the number of nails in the ceiling. Mindless punishment but harmless.

Still adrift on the syllabus there was a lot of catching up to do. Had I been shown a map of the world, I couldn't have located either

Africa or England, but I could have drawn a colourful map of the Orinoco basin, and discussed tapioca and the Gulf stream. In history we studied the appalling behaviour of the Spanish *conquistadors* like Pizarro and Cortes in South America, where they robbed and slaughtered the unfortunate natives who just wanted to get on with their lives and rip each other's living hearts out. And yet English history was entirely ignored.

Since I was very young I had walked with a slight limp. Nobody knew why. My legs frequently hurt if I ran or climbed steps. I'd recently had a serious horse-riding accident that had left me with chronic back pain. Although I enjoyed tennis and netball I wasn't much of a swimmer. Our gym mistress wore a short white tunic and very dirty knickers, disagreeably visible when our gym lessons involved lying on the floor. Unlike almost all the other girls in my class, I could not balance on the bar without falling off, could not do a backwards somersault or handstand, could not climb a rope, spring, bounce, leap, dangle by my ankles or hang from my ears. I definitely couldn't vault over the horse because my legs didn't bend at the hips as they should. Why it should have been quite so important to this woman that I should vault the horse I've no idea, but it frustrated her enormously that each time I ran up the slope towards it and grabbed the handles, my legs caught on the suede body and I either fell backwards, or once or twice slithered over and onto my head. When the horse had reached its highest level she made me crouch on it between the handles so the more athletic girls could use my bent back to bounce off. It was really quite painful, but less distressing than being made to try and vault the damned thing again and again. Eight years later, X-rays revealed a cracked pelvis and damaged coccyx, a crushed vertebral disc, and my lower spine was simultaneously twisted on its axis and bent sideways. I don't think all the pounding from my classmates had done it much good.

Apart from English and French lessons that I loved and where I was the teacher's favourite, I was multi-untalented and never going to be a star pupil. But I tried hard, because more than anything except news of my mother, I wanted my father's approval. Whenever I looked into his face, all I ever saw was disappointment.

94

# Chapter Thirteen

# Home Truth

One evening when I was alone in the house I had opened a desk drawer to look for something and came across a half-written letter from Helen to her sister. I flicked through it, and at the top of a page read 'unpleasant and difficult girl, but Bob'(my father) 'says she can't be as black as she's painted'. I felt sick and put the letter back into the drawer. I didn't want to read any more. That was me. *Who was painting me black? Why? What had I done wrong?* The only two sins I was consciously aware of were helping myself to a teaspoonful of Ribena, one of many things reserved exclusively for the baby but which I couldn't resist occasionally, or forgetting to wipe out the bath after I'd shaved my legs. There had been complaints about that a few times. They seemed trivial sins to warrant being painted black.

I knew I wasn't perfect but I really didn't think I was bad. I'd renounced the stealing habit years before, except for the sips of Ribena. I hadn't any recollection of ever hurting or attacking anybody. But from the day my father had collected me from Granny's house when I'd stood with the toothpaste-scented hair, I'd had an uncomfortable feeling, and it is still there now, that everybody knew something unspeakably dreadful that I had done, and that only I didn't know about. It may be why, ever since, from time to time I dream that I'm being hunted by the police for a murder I'd committed long ago and forgotten about. I recalled Nan telling me about one of my little classmates from Hanworth. She had been killed when a snowball with a stone in it hit her on the head. I began to wonder, later. *Had I thrown the snowball? Had I killed my friend?*

Helen was bathing the baby one evening, and I was sitting in the bathroom chatting, tipping water from the bath over the baby's shoulders from a plastic cup. Helen pulled the plug, and as the water ran away I filled the cup from the tap, and tipped it. The baby was laughing, and then suddenly squealed. Helen snatched her out of the bath.

"Get away from her," she shouted. "Don't you ever touch her again. How dare you pour hot water over her!" I opened my mouth and closed it like a fish, trying to say that I hadn't realised the water was starting to run hot, but Helen had already stomped out of the room clutching the baby tightly to her chest. She left behind her a look of such hatred. I would never again touch the baby or be comfortable alone with her.

My father knocked on my bedroom door one Friday morning to get me up to go to school, but I was awake already, and had been throughout the night with a terrible stomach ache. As I sat up in bed an excruciating pain shot through me.

"Daddy, there's something wrong. My stomach hurts so badly."

"Come on, Sue, get up and get ready."

I shuffled to the door and opened it.

"Daddy, it's really bad. I can't stand up."

"Get dressed," he said wearily.

I tried to get into my school uniform as the pain intensified, and I heard him say to Helen: "She probably hasn't done her homework and is trying to get out of going to school."

I climbed back into bed and tried to rock away the pain, fighting waves of nausea. And wondering why he thought I hadn't done my homework. I always did it.

In the corridor I heard them talking, and then the closing of the front door and the car driving away.

After half an hour Helen came into the room and stood looking down at me. She felt my head, and said: "Where is the pain?"

I pointed to my stomach.

"Let me smell your breath."

I breathed towards her.

Then she walked out of the room and I heard her talking on the telephone.

A doctor arrived half an hour later, and then an ambulance.

By mid-day I was in the operating theatre of Nairobi hospital having my appendix removed.

When Helen and my father came to visit that afternoon, they bought books and flowers and a tin of toffees, and my father told some of his best jokes. Laughing hurt, but despite the pain I felt triumphant; they'd been proved wrong about me. What I would really have liked would have been for Daddy to say he was sorry for doubting me.

Socially I was very happy at school and was able to build a new circle of friends, something that had so often been destroyed by changing schools and countries. You needed to have at least one reliable friend at Delamere, because for some unfathomable reason the lavatory doors had no locks on them. To guarantee privacy you had to either sit with your feet pushed hard against the door from the inside – tricky, or have your friend stand outside for the duration of your visit.

It wouldn't be quite true to say they were the best days of my life, but certainly Delamere Girls High School wasn't a bad place to be and my days there progressed at an even pace.

At home I tried very hard to do nothing that could be interpreted as unpleasant. I'd sit in my room, reading or watching the weaver birds in the pepper tree, whose shiny red clusters of berries rustled pleasingly when they were stirred by a breeze. My secret friend, an enormous rat with a glossy dark brown coat and an intelligent enquiring eye, sat on the window sill looking in at me looking out. Sometimes I put out a little chocolate or other titbit for him, and watched as he sat delicately nibbling it from his little front paws, and then meticulously polishing his face and whiskers. He was the nearest thing to the pet I wanted so much.

# Chapter Fourteen

## The Day of Eggs

Everybody we knew had an African house-servant and/or cook, but at that time we didn't. Helen was terrified of Africans: she regarded them all as bloodthirsty savages infested with unpleasant parasites and incurable tropical diseases, and very dirty too. She did her own housework and her own cooking and when my father came home from work, he helped with the dishes.

Helen was an excellent cook. Her repertoire was small and basic, but everything she made was faultless. Pastry was light and golden. Chicken was moistly succulent beneath a perfectly crisped skin. Vegetables retained their natural colours and textures. Her apple crumble could never be equalled. Each meal was calculated with a frugality that would have made Scrooge seem a spendthrift. Over a period of about a month, the two pints of milk that were delivered daily were tainted, due, I think, to some peculiar plant that the cattle had been eating. The flavour was really very unpleasant, but having assured herself that it was not harmful to our health, Helen insisted that my father and I used it all up. We shouldn't let it go to waste, although she and the baby were exempted.

Everybody had a precisely adequate meal, perfectly cooked and delicious, yet she had no more confidence in her abilities as a cook than she did in herself generally. She was very informed about nutrition, making sure all meals were correctly balanced, that we had all the right vitamins and not too much cholesterol, and this was decades before the advent of 'healthy eating'. There were no leftovers, and very rarely a second helping, and generally we were all slim and healthy.

The trigger for a cataclysmic row one Saturday lunchtime was an omelette. My day had begun perfectly, with a long riding lesson. Daddy worked on Saturday mornings, and he picked me up from where Major Blackwell deposited his pupils. We drove home together. There was no uncomfortable atmosphere in the house. It was quiet and calm. We were eating and Helen and my father were chatting. However, my omelette was slightly undercooked, leaving an area of glutinous gel where the white was not set sufficiently, with little curly white strings in it. It's one of the very few things that I just cannot eat. It wasn't much, no more than a couple of teaspoons. As unobtrusively as possible I smeared it around the plate and covered it with my knife and fork.

"Finish your food," Helen said in her deceptively gentle voice.

"I have."

"I told you to finish your food. You've left some on the plate."

"No, I haven't."

"You have left some omelette on your plate. I want you to finish it."

My father joined in.

"Come on Sue, eat up."

The blackberry incident flashed back and my mind filled with the memory of being forced to shovel squirmy maggots into my mouth. I was not going to be forced again to eat something that would make me retch. Even the thought made me gag, but both Helen and my father angrily insisted that I was to finish what was on my plate.

Eventually I blurted out: "I'm sorry, I can't eat that bit. It's not cooked properly."

Her face scarlet, Helen pushed her chair back, burst into sobs and slammed out of the room, followed by my father. I sat gazing at the offending plate and wondering what to do next. *Why was it so important to eat the small amount of inedible egg? Did two teaspoons of undercooked egg white warrant quite such a drama?*

As nothing else happened I went to my room from where I could hear Helen shouting about my rebellious behaviour.

The more I thought about it, the more resentful I felt. As far as I could see I did nothing wrong, was polite, and tried to be as self-effacing as possible, but it wasn't good enough. I simply didn't know what else to try, besides which I was tired of having to try all the time. So I decided to leave home and make my way in the world. I had just had my thirteenth birthday.

I walked the several miles into Nairobi town centre, with no money and no idea of what would happen next, but a determination not to go back to where I would have to eat undercooked egg white. After wandering around for a couple of hours by which time dusk was starting to fall, I began feeling a certain anxiety. I hadn't any idea what to do, having no money, but I would not go home. I sat in the doorway of a local cinema, feeling hungry and attracting quite a lot of curious attention from the people coming out. I thought, this is what beggars feel like, those poor bundles of rags who live in doorways like this one, never knowing when or what or even if they will eat again, with no home, no bed, no clean clothes. I started to feel as sorry for myself as I did for them.

The urine-soaked alleys of Nairobi were no place for a teenage European girl alone at night. The country was still in a State of Emergency and Europeans never wandered around the backstreets of the town. They weren't safe. At this time there was a Scottish regiment, the Cameronian (Scottish Rifles) based just outside Nairobi. They had a fearsome reputation as foul-mouthed, heavy drinking, hard-fisted characters. It was a rare week when the local newspapers didn't report a bar smashed up, or an outbreak of drunken fisticuffs leaving half a dozen participants bruised and battered. I was crouching in the dirty doorway with no idea at all what to do next, when a short khaki-clad figure stopped in front of me.

"Was it a good film?" gargled a broad Scottish accent.

"I don't know. I didn't go in."

"Would you like a cup of coffee and something to eat?"

I accepted with shocking eagerness, ready to pay whatever price necessary to get out of this doorway and have a meal and fellow human being to talk to.

We wandered around companionably looking in shop windows and ended up at a smoky little dive in a side street. The menu offered

100

fried egg baps, tea or coffee. I opted for a coffee and the bap. Never has food tasted better: the egg-white lacy, crisp and golden without a trace of transparent slime, the yolk hot and runny, the floury bap soft and springy, and with lashings of brown sauce. The sandwiches were so good we had a second round.

While we ate my new friend asked what I was doing around town, at night, alone, at the age of 13. I explained about Helen and her bloody omelette, and said I wasn't going home, definitely. I wondered if he knew somewhere I could stay temporarily until I found a job. He said he'd see what he could do, and disappeared for a few moments. Then we resumed our patrol of the late night streets, and it did seem to me that I was being steered in a very definite direction. The blue flashing lights that slammed to a halt beside me said it all. My new friend had shopped me. Two carloads of police marched towards us. They asked him his name, and fed him into one of the cars.

"Now, young lady, could you tell us what your name is?"

"Marilyn Monroe."

"OK Marilyn, in the car."

They fed me into the second car, and we sped off to the Police Station. I never saw the young soldier again to say goodbye, nor to thank him, and I never learned his name. So much for the frightening reputation of the Cameronian (Scottish Rifles). He more than likely saved my life, and almost certainly from a fate worse than death. Driving towards the station I felt not only privately very relieved, but also quite triumphant. Not only the soldier, but all these policemen and no doubt others knew how unreasonable Helen could be over an uneaten teaspoon of viscous egg white. That made me feel pretty good. I thought that in future she would have to behave a great deal better if she didn't want to find herself getting a very bad reputation.

A fatherly policeman gave me a talk about letting someone know next time I was going to be staying out late, and then handed me over to my silent father who drove me home. I declined to apologise to Helen, and we all spent a week of not talking to each other.

Oh, and another baby was on the way.

# Chapter Fifteen

# Machakos

School holidays appeared on the horizon.

Living in Kenya was not like living in Europe, the United States or anywhere in a high density residential neighbourhood and/or anywhere there is a public transport system. Everything was far away, and children were dependant upon their parents for transport. The nearest of my schoolfriends lived six miles away on the other side of Nairobi, others even further. There was no means of reaching them unless my father drove me there and collected me, and he couldn't do that during weekdays because he was at work. It looked as if Helen and I were going to be stuck with each other's company for the long duration of the summer holidays, a depressing prospect for both of us.

Then my father told me I was going to spend six weeks on a farm about fifty miles from Nairobi. That was the beginning of one of the happiest periods of my life.

John and Penny Shaw were ranchers who lived with their two young children in a single-storey farmhouse built around an inner grass courtyard at Konza in the Machakos district. During the school holidays they opened their relaxed home to half a dozen children whose parents, for whatever reason, sent them there knowing they would be happy, safe and well-looked after. The weeks spent there were a period of unrestricted adventure and primitive pleasure. We could run wild and free. There was no electricity. Charcoal fuelled the oven and heated the water. The servants ironed the laundry with heavy cast-iron flatirons, the lower half filled with glowing coals, and at night they lit kerosene lamps. We ate enormously, starting with breakfasts of porridge, eggs, steaks and toast, through huge lunches and three-course dinners. The energy we expended required a lot of fuelling.

We swam in the borehole, stalked each other Indian-style on our bellies through the bush. We wrestled and raced, and occasionally woke at 4.00am to drive out into the bush to watch the African herdsmen milking the cattle into scrubbed oil cans. By the light of kerosene lamps, their hands smothered in what looked like axle grease, they squished the foamy milk from bulging udders, singing tunelessly as they did so. The milk pinged against the sides of the cans, and the waiting cattle lowed and moved about in the darkness around us. We also hunted game for the table, to my eternal shame, going out about once a week to shoot a gazelle, or occasionally a zebra. But only ever for food. Nobody killed animals in the name of sport.

The African bush was untamed and wild, a vast playground for a raggedy rough and tumble group of kids as we were. In the evenings we played charades, cards and crazy games involving blowing feathers and ping pong balls to score goals. A favourite game was packing a pudding basin with flour, then turning it out onto a board. Penny stuck a sweet on top, in the middle. In turn we each had to cut a slice of the flour 'cake'.It could be as big or small slice as you wished, but if it made the cake collapse you had to pick out the sweet from the heap of flour with your mouth. We listened to music on the radio, and to spooky stories read by the flickering lamp light. It was a glorious contrast to the restrained lifestyle at home. The only rule was that you never pointed a gun, loaded or unloaded, at another person.

We sliced the tips of our fingers to draw blood, and swore oaths of eternal friendship; dug thorns and splinters from ourselves and each other; went on snake-hunting expeditions in pursuit of puff adders, mambas, cobras and pythons. Fortunately we never found anything larger than a very small python that slithered away into a hole. More successful safaris involved catching the rose beetles that preyed on the roses trying so hard to grow in the dusty heat. Penny paid a bounty for any of these pests we caught. Family life there was my idea of perfection. Happiness, love, care, fun, laughter. To me this was the family life I dreamed of, and secretly I pretended John and Penny were my parents.

John's parents, Sir Robert de Vere Shaw and his wife Joan lived a little way down the hill in a lovely old farmhouse filled with antique furniture and rugs. Joan always wore a rust-coloured trousered safari suit, her long grey hair scooped up into a loose bun, with a perpetual cigarette burning from a long holder. Kindly, bluff Sir Robert with his bushy moustache only seemed to have one pair of trousers, of well-worn green corduroy secured around his waist with an old regimental tie, worn with a checked shirt with rolled-up sleeves and an elderly sweat-stained wide-brimmed hat. They were the most hospitable and generous people imaginable. Their hunters and polo ponies were stabled behind the house, and those are the horses we rode – all fit and spirited, and it was a rare week when one or other of us didn't hit the red dust at high speed.

I floated on cloud nine, especially having daily access to the horses. We galloped over open plains and rode over the hurdles of the point-to-point course, raced up and down the polo ground whacking at the wooden ball with polo sticks (although I lagged far behind everybody else until somebody pointed out that you hit the ball with the long side of the stick, and not the little end, which is all but impossible at the gallop).

Poaching was rife, giraffe and zebra killed for no more than the hair of their tails to make into bracelets. Led by John we chased poachers through the scrub, lashing at them with leather whips and screaming like banshees, sending them stampeding in fear.

As the oldest of the children there I enjoyed the privilege of occasionally staying the night down the hill with John's parents. John or Penny would drive me down to the house in the early evening, where I would have a bath in the rusty-coloured water before changing into my pyjamas and dressing gown. Dinner at the senior Shaw's was a formal affair, despite my nightwear. The house-servant served our meals at a stately table in the grand candle-lit dining room. From numerous oil paintings on the walls the eyes of fierce previous baronets watched. Never having dined in formal style

I found the etiquette confusing. The first time I was served soup was particularly baffling. We all had bowls set in front of us, and then the servant came around with a tray containing a collection of slightly larger bowls filled with soup. I took one of these bowls and stood it in the bowl that was on the table in front of me; the servant remained standing patiently by my side. Obviously I was meant to do something, but what? Gulp down the soup quickly so he could serve the next person? That seemed very rude. Joan explained that I should pour some of the soup from bowl No. 1 into bowl No. 2, and return bowl No. 1 to the tray. Ever since, I have wondered why.

After we had eaten we moved to the sitting room where Smith and Robinson, the family dachshunds snored and twitched their short legs in front of a log fire. Joan poured tea from a silver pot suspended in a silver cradle over a spirit lamp, and then we played canasta by the firelight. Those evenings remain a treasured memory of complete contentment and a wish that time would stand still at that moment.

Sir Robert owned a magnificent, very large dark bay mare called Jennifer, a Da Vinci creation with a powerful arched neck and curvy bouncing rump. Jennifer never walked. She danced on her hooves in an exquisite ballet, her chin curved into her chest with flecks of spume lathering her mouth and between her hind legs. Her provocative buttocks rose and dipped to the rhythm of her gait, and dark patches of sweat stained her chest and flanks.

More than anything, I wanted to ride Jennifer, to feel her muscly power. Sir Robert climbed off her on one of our daily hacks, and handed me the reins.

"Just be sensible," he smiled, and climbed onto my vacant mount, a lanky dapple-grey polo pony called Judy, that I loved dearly.

I hauled myself aboard glowing with pride, and rode Jennifer happily and easily along the paths through the bush on a long loose rein. She cantered slowly, like a rocking horse. I'd never ridden any horse so big and powerful and was feeling pleased with myself and completely at ease. All should have ended well, had not a horrible jealous boy kicked his horse into a gallop and shot past, walloping Jennifer on her huge bottom. She set off at full tilt. As I'd been sitting slackly relaxed there was no time to collect her before she was in a pounding gallop and completely beyond my control. I turned her in a circle to slow her, but we were on a hillside and as the circle began to face downhill, propelled by her own weight she gathered ever more momentum. She was careering hell for leather when she stumbled. We parted company. I became airborne for some time before hitting the ground with a loud thump and crack, and remembered nothing more.

Faces peered down to where I lay tucked into cool white sheets in a primitive hospital. A doctor tickled the unresponsive soles of my feet, tapped my knees with a small rubber mallet, flexed my legs backwards and forwards, and shook his head. For two days I lay there in the bed wondering what would happen, praying that I wouldn't have to go home. Gradually the feeling came back into my legs, and I could walk again, a little sore and shaky, but mobile once more. I went back to the farm and the daily adventures, although I would never be allowed to ride Jennifer again. The legacy of that ride has been chronic back pain throughout my life; but I haven't any regrets.

John's wife Penny's parents, the Milbanks, were a handsome couple who like Sir Robert were both descended from a long line of baronets. So many of the 'Old Kenya' families were connected to the English aristocracy. The British community included an impressive number of Dukes and Lords. The Milbanks lived nearby with a tribe of enchanting Pekinese dogs. Penny's younger sister Susan was one of the most talented show-jumpers in Kenya. Her small grey mare, Lili Marlene, was a horse of immense courage who would tackle seemingly impossible fences and fly over them. She was a favourite with the crowds and her entrance into the ring was usually accompanied by the song after which she was named.

All we children lived and were treated as part of the family, driving bumpily around in a rattling Land Rover, over rutted dirt tracks and through deep drifts called *dongas*. We visited neighbouring white farmers, spent evenings at the rustic polo club with its *makuti[6]* roof, watching films, plays and the adults dressed in nightwear riding midnight steeplechases. I was not aware then that most of the people we met daily had their names written into the history books of Kenya. They were the first pioneering families to have arrived in the country and transported themselves and their possessions to their new homes by ox carts.

A nearby farm we regularly visited belonged to Philip Percival, one of the first and last of the 'great white hunters'. He lived there with his son Richard, who was a rancher. Ernest Hemingway had hunted with him in 1933. The rather dark and gloomy house was crammed with trophies; heads hung from the walls and skins draped the furniture and covered the floor. They were kind and hospitable people who gave us tea and cakes and showed us around their stables. At dusk they took us to the dried riverbed where, from a cave, clouds of bats erupted.

Weatherworn, wiry, tough, hard-working and easy-going, these folk dressed for comfort. The regulation dress for the men was open-necked cotton shirts with rolled up sleeves, suede or leather ankle boots, khaki knee-high socks and rather long, baggy khaki shorts. They didn't wear anything under the shorts. This was no secret, because they tended to sit with one ankle casually resting on the other knee, leaving a generous gap between cloth and flesh.

These were tough men and women who loved the magnificent country that they had done so much to develop, and who knew that their idyllic colonial existence was almost over. Their parents had settled in the harsh land and built rambling, elegant timber homes, furnished with family heirlooms; they had battled disease, natural disaster, wild animals and problems with the natives. They drove battered Land Rovers or pickups, and their Sunday best was their least tattered clothes. Their skins were white, but in their hearts they were African. They loved the country, and they loved the African people. The farms employed large numbers of workers, all of whom were cared for, fed, housed, and whose numerous wives, mothers, sisters, aunts, children, chickens and goats had the run of the estate. And there was a reciprocal affection towards the whites from many of the Africans.

The reactionary view of all whites as wicked imperialist exploiters was unfair. No doubt there were exceptions, but I believe the majority of the white settlers were genuinely fond of their workers and regarded them as an extension of their family. African children were educated and the old and sick looked after, in many instances by white employers who strictly speaking had no responsibility for these dependants of their employees. This was 'old Kenya', peopled by the early British settlers who had developed the country, the pioneers, a dying breed whose world was changing as African independence grew ever closer. The Europeans like us who had come to settle in Kenya after the war were 'New Kenyans'.

My heart grew a little heavier with each day that died in the dust under the Machakos sun, as the inevitable return home drew closer. On the final day I stood masochistically by the doorway, watching the long straight road in the far distance for the moving cloud of dust that signalled the approach of my father's car. No matter how I tried, no matter how many times I was told I would soon be coming back, I couldn't stop weeping. I just wept and sobbed, and sobbed and wept until I was quite soggy and exhausted. While I was mourning the loss of this unspoiled existence, Helen interpreted it as a direct attack on her, a demonstration of how much I hated her and didn't want to live with her. I tried hard not to display my misery, but the tight silent stare and the frigid atmosphere just made everything worse. Several days of unspeaking mealtimes and sudden disappearing acts would pass before life in our house returned to what passed for normal. I counted the days until my next stay at the farm.

In August 1960 Penny was expecting a new baby. John was a Captain in the Kenya Regiment. He was a 'man's man', universally popular with everybody who knew him. At the same time he was patient and kind to his young guests and like Penny went out of his way to entertain us. We all adored him. Occasionally he went away briefly on regimental duties, taking with him an African driver. I remember the previous year that we had requested the radio station to play *When Johnny Comes Marching Home Again* for him.

I'd had a wonderful stay on the farm that summer and had only been home a few weeks. While we were eating our evening meal, the news came on the radio. A white Kenyan farmer had been killed in a road accident. It was John Shaw, 30 years old, leaving Penny a widow with three children under the age of 4, including a one-month-old baby. The African driver who should have driven him home was drunk, so John drove himself. He failed to see the sand lorry parked on the road in the dark with no lights and drove straight into it. He died instantly. The driver was unharmed.

The loss to his family and friends was beyond measure, and mine was no less. I had idolised him, and I just did not know how to cope at the thought I would never see him again. I knew it was the end of those carefree days at Machakos. Mummy had gone. Minetta had gone. Daddy was out of reach. Nan was more than 4,000 miles away. John was gone. The farm days were gone. *When was it going to end?*

Our family's new social circle consisted of eight people, all ex-nurses and their families. They were normal and friendly folk, who always made a great fuss of me, and I was aware that they were making a particular effort so that I would enjoy myself. Unlike Helen they were confident and relaxed, and maybe they knew that life with her wasn't easy and suspected she was rather heavy-handed with the black paint.

Life at home wasn't a constant state of war. There were sometimes long periods when we all seemed to get along well. Helen and I went to the cinema together; she took me to buy new clothes and shoes and to visit her friends for coffee mornings. She tried, I'm quite sure. But just as I thought we'd arrived at an understanding and could be friends, some unknown deed or incautious word sent us back to the bottom of the ladder.

We were often invited out for long Sunday lunches, or barbecues. These were happy events where everybody sprawled on rugs in the afternoon sun, laughing and drinking lager from tall glasses frosted with condensation. The children and babies played and crawled together in the shade of the jacaranda trees under the watchful eyes of their *ayahs*, African nannies. Only Helen couldn't relax; she didn't want black people touching her children and giving them terrible diseases, and regardless of the gentle assurances of her friends, she was rigid with anxiety for as long as there was a black face near her offspring.

Our closest family friends were a couple with two young boys and a handsome dog called Pel, a Rhodesian Ridgeback. Pel was enormous and gentle and I spent many happy hours playing with him. They lived in a large bungalow on a coffee farm in the Thika area, and visits to them were always a treat because the atmosphere there was warm and relaxed, and Irene baked what were unquestionably the best jam tarts in the world. Meals with them were most satisfying because the food was accompanied by uninhibited conversation and laughter.Her husband, John, was a slender, tanned man who paid me special attention, driving me around the hundreds of acres of the estate on the back of his motorbike; he had suffered from a difficult and unhappy relationship with his step-mother and I think he knew how it felt.

Suddenly those visits stopped. I missed them and wondered what had happened, but asking was not an option because of the tacit non-talking rule under which we lived.

It was about a year before they resurfaced, and Irene invited me to stay with them for a few days. While I was there she told me there had been a fierce argument between my father and John, who had wanted to give me a puppy like Pel because he thought it would be good for me. He recognised my hunger for something to love. My father had taken exception to the suggestion that I needed a puppy. There had been an almighty row and it had taken a long cooling down period before they were ready to put the incident behind them.

While Irene was telling me this my mind went back to an incident that had happened all those years ago before we left England, when we used to spend our summer holidays at Boscombe. One afternoon as we walked back to the guesthouse there was another person with us, a man who seemed to be a friend of my parents. They were laughing together. We paused at the window of a toyshop from where a most appealing small bear reached out with imploring furry arms hoping, I knew, that he could be mine. We stared at each other with mutual longing, and the man who was with us wanted to buy the bear for me. I wanted him to buy the bear for me, and knew that when my father said the man was not to buy me the bear, it was just

110

a joke. Why wouldn't he want me to have that small bear to add to the collection on the window sill in my bedroom at home? We all stood and stared at the bear for a few moments. Something had gone wrong because my father and the man were exchanging cold, angry words, and then we were walking away, on up the road to the guesthouse. I looked back at the bear's sad face, hoping that the man had gone into the shop to buy him, but he was walking quickly in the opposite direction. For the rest of our holiday I fully expected the bear would turn up sooner or later: either tucked up on my pillow, sitting at the breakfast table, or perhaps peering out from my bucket. It wasn't until we returned home to Hanworth I finally accepted that I wasn't going to see the bear ever again, and I never understood why.

The downside of all these lovely interludes and meals we enjoyed at friends' houses was that Helen felt she had to reciprocate. Inviting anybody to our house was torture for her, an event that would be agonised over for many weeks. Firstly there was the cost. She came from a poor mining family and even though my father earned a handsome salary and we had two new cars, she fretted over the cost of everything. She had no confidence in herself as a cook or hostess, despite the fact that every meal she prepared was always cooked to perfection and every scrap eaten with relish and compliments (apart from the single incident of the egg). Not only did she feel she was not up to the job, but her other dilemma was how much to cook. Should she allow one medium potato per person, or two small ones? There was never any question of anybody having a large potato. It was two small or one medium. But which? She would torment herself for weeks over that simple question, and wonder whether one small tin of peas was sufficient between four people or whether it should be supplemented with one or two carrots. The starter would be soup, which could be designed to provide a precisely calculated serving per person. Dessert was similarly manageable, but the question of the vegetable portions caused untold anguish and sleepless nights.

This strange complex made her life unnecessarily fraught. Many of us may worry about whether our culinary talents will let us down, but a handful of peas, or a few potatoes didn't really seem to justify such angst. For some years I assumed it was to do with cost. I thought potatoes were a luxury until I was married and learning to keep house. I was astonished to learn just how cheap they were.

Entertaining was an ordeal, not a pleasure for her. Although she thought the world of her friends, visitors really weren't welcome. They were a lot of work, and you didn't know how long they would stay and whether they would like the food and it would be a relief when they left. Every time we were invited anywhere she needed reassurance that we weren't a nuisance, that our hosts really did want us to visit. And however much she was reassured, she couldn't be persuaded. This gave me a complex that I still have. Walking into anybody's house, even my own children or closest friends, there is always that feeling at the back of my mind that I am putting them out, imposing on them. I have to force myself to appear relaxed and comfortable when my instinct is to leave quickly.

In 1960 my father had been promoted to Managing Director, and bought a handsome and elegant house in one of Nairobi's most sought-after residential areas, Riverside Drive. From necessity there was a gardener – with the house came gardens of nearly two acres, terraced down to a length of winding river. The first terrace was an emerald lawn maintained by regular sprinkling. The next terrace was also lawn, with two huge specimen palm trees. Then came a hedge of brilliant red waxy hibiscus. A formal rose garden followed, and so it went on, ending finally in a copse of rustling eucalyptus trees bordering our stretch of the river, where I once came upon an Asian family picnicking.

Never must the gardener, an elderly grey-haired and wrinkled man step over the threshold of the kitchen door into the house. He represented a clear and present danger of something. Disease, theft, rape, murder? The poor man went about his task of keeping the garden in perfect condition, whistling monotonously and continuously, just like the garden boy had done all those years ago in the garden at Lower Kabete Road. If he needed advice he had to knock loudly on the back door, or hover in the driveway until my father came home.

112

I think my father must have managed to dismantle Helen's dislike of household pets, because a white fluffy cat joined the family, and a cross-bred Alsatian called Rex who was allowed inside the house (but only in the living room) in the evenings when we watched television.

Helen never seemed to be wholly well. Sometimes it was her back, wrecked, she said, by years of nursing; at other times her kidneys or migraine. I think much of it was due to the fact that she lived such in a constant state of stress and anxiety. The least disruption in the precarious equilibrium in our household would trigger a new attack of something and she would snap that she was having to take barbiturates. I hadn't any idea what a barbiturate was, but it sounded pretty serious. Then we would walk very quietly and talk, on those rare occasions that we did, in lowered tones. Finally, because she just wasn't up to managing a large house, with two small children (the second baby was another little girl) and the difficult step-daughter, she reluctantly agreed we should have a house-servant to do the cleaning and laundry, and wash the dishes. But he was not on any account to touch our food. It must have been purgatory for her living in a country where she was so afraid of the native population, who were all around us, all the time, wherever we went.

I can only think some great personal tragedy had led her to leaving England and coming to live and work in a country where she was so perpetually anxious.

What was disconcerting was the way in which things could change without warning. One moment everything was peaceful and the next a tumult. There was no mild tremor, no tinkling glass, no whisper of a breeze to announce the attack. Like a shark, Helen seemed to cruise beneath the apparently calm surface waters of my life, waiting, it seemed, for an opportunity to strike, accusing, threatening, weeping. She was constantly on the alert for an insult, and found hidden meaning in innocent remarks. A careless comment would fly like a spark onto a tinder and cause an explosion. I might say without thinking that the mother of one of my friends was very pretty, or had beautiful hair, or was a marvellous cook. Helen would interpret this to mean that she herself was none of these things, and

113

would stump in her ungainly way out of the room, red-faced and tight-lipped, leaving my father and myself each in our own silences. *Caveat orator*.

She cultivated her inferiority complex like a prize plant, and wore a permanently martyred expression. Although she would never have been beautiful, she could if she had tried just a little have been quite striking. She had large grey eyes fringed by black lashes, well-defined dark eyebrows, an aquiline nose, a wide mouth and strong chin and perfect skin. Big-boned, had she carried herself upright she would have looked handsome. Instead she walked with a strange listing motion, her right elbow jammed onto her right hip and her hand up near her chin as if towing an invisible sled behind her. Her hair was thin and straight and grey, but cut well could have looked chic. She wore shapeless dresses to just above ankle height, and flat, sensible sandals. She didn't shave her legs. Everything about her screamed silently: "I'm a decent modest woman. I don't flaunt myself." Not like Mummy, then.

Her catchphrase was "Of course, I'm only a *second* wife," as if that was somehow someone else's fault. She was the opposite of my vivacious and cheerful mother who was pretty and curvy, with hazel eyes so light and so bright that they appeared gold.

Although she had a gentle, soft musical voice every word sounded as if it had been thoroughly processed before it was allowed out. Conversation didn't flow, but came out in spurts, like a series of geysers in sporadic eruption.

Instead of seeing me as the catalyst who had transformed her from spinster nurse into wife and mother thanks to my troublesome hands, she was so tormented by jealousy of my mother that I represented a permanent reminder of her predecessor, whom she still regarded as her rival. There was very little I could do about that, apart from living elsewhere, but there wasn't an available elsewhere to live.

The unspoken rule within the family seemed to be that nobody spoke. Displeasure was transmitted by atmosphere. Walking into the house I would instantly feel that something was wrong. An icy miasma filled every corner. I would know that I was invariably the cause, but however much I burrowed into the crevices of my mind

114

searching for the careless word, wrong facial expression or some sin of omission, I never found the answer. Something was amiss, there was no doubt about that, but nothing was said. My father withdrew further into himself, the little girl stared at me white-faced and open-mouthed, and Helen emanated fury. This could last for a few days and the relief when the atmosphere warmed up was tainted by a lingering frustration at having no idea at all what had caused it. And then came the constant anxiety as to when the next episode would start, as it inevitably would.

Nobody spoke, you see.

No-one said: "Look, I'm really angry about..."

Nobody said: "I want a word with you."

Nobody asked: "Why did you do..."

We just didn't. On those occasions when the atmosphere was chilly, we simply kept quiet with our own thoughts and waited, through silent meals and evenings silently watching television, the silence broken only by the occasional moist slurping of my father's pipe, or Rex slobbering over his genitals. Helen could barely stand to be in the same room with me, it was palpable. With the benefit of many years gone by, I recognise that we were incompatible because we both shared a supreme lack of self-confidence. She had no belief in herself any more than I did. To her I was a constant reminder that my father had had another wife. For my part I didn't dislike her. I certainly didn't hate her. It was her coldness that made it impossible for me, with my own securities and lack of confidence, to approach her with any warmth. I imagine that she did her best, and had I been more sure of myself and felt some support from my father, we might have found a way to get along. But we couldn't and didn't.

Family life was like sitting in a chilly room with an electric coal-effect fire without the heating on; you could see flames, but there wasn't any warmth. One evening I suddenly found the noise of my father's pipe, and the licking dog intolerable. My entire skin ached, my jaw clenched, and I wanted to scream. But of course I didn't. Instead I shuffled my feet around and clicked my tongue to try to drown out the sounds that were making me feel murderously angry. My father told me to stop fidgeting and keep quiet. I excused myself and went to my room to read. This intense reaction to noise is now known as misophonia, and it can be triggered by any number of sounds, but is most often a reaction to the noise of people eating.

# Chapter Sixteen

# Cinderella

Horses and horse-riding were my passions. I thought about almost nothing else, and I dreamed of having my own horse. A school friend had just been given a pony that she kept at the stables at the end of Riverside Drive, and I spent most of my spare time with her. Probably I talked about it too much, because over dinner one evening Helen snapped: "You're miserable because you don't have a horse. I didn't even have a warm coat when I was your age."

"I bet you had your own mother," I shouted. When pushed hard enough, I fought back.

I kept trying to think how I could possibly buy my own horse, and scoured the pages of the newspaper daily. One day I saw an advertisement, and I can clearly see it now. 'Wanted. Horse for 14-year-old girl. Also hack'.

Two things I knew instantly. 'Hack' was a mis-spelling of 'tack', and the 14-year-old girl was me.

The words ran through my head for days, until my father announced that Helen had been saving money from her housekeeping (which my father gave her), to buy me a pony. My father would pay the monthly livery bill at the local stables. Every waking minute I thought about that pony, and I made myself a silent promise: I would be a model student, daughter, step-daughter and half-sister, further beyond reproach than Caesar's wife. Nobody, ever, anywhere was going to be able to paint me black again.

There were two replies to the advertisement. Knowing nothing at all about buying a horse, all we had to rely on was my personal choice, and I did have a good eye for conformation. We looked first at a lanky flea-bitten grey known to be a good jumper, and another pony, also a flea-bitten grey, an Arab-Somali cross called Cinderella, a sparky and unpredictable ride.

Unlike the first pony which was just a couple of miles from where we lived, Cinderella was over 60 miles from Nairobi. She belonged to an English family living on a farm at a barren place called Kajiado in the Maasai homelands. The drive there was long, hot, dusty and bumpy over a stony track. I gave Cinderella my heart at first sight. I loved her as I had never loved anything before, instantly and overwhelmingly. She was saddled up so that I could have a trial ride. Before my feet were in the stirrups she'd taken off, and carted me where she wished at a full-tilt gallop, jerking to a jarring halt just before she seemed intent upon leaping over the farmhouse. By the time she had run out of steam we were both bathed in mingled sweat and heaving from exhilaration. She cost £60. That was quite a lot of money in 1961.

There were two weeks until the last day of term, when she would travel by train to her new home. One of the grooms from the livery yard would collect her and take her to the stables to await my arrival after school.

How intolerably slowly those two weeks passed, trying all the time to make sure my behaviour was impeccable, hardly daring to speak for fear of saying the wrong thing, but at the same time not wanting to appear sullen by not speaking and having the pony delivery cancelled.

So that I could travel independently from home to the stables and to school, part of the deal was that I should save up to buy a bicycle, which I did. This hateful contraption left me with a life-long loathing of bicycles in general and that bicycle in particular. It was invested with a malevolent spirit. At weekends it made the journey between home and the stables efficiently. But during the weekdays it produced a daily catalogue of deflations, punctures, detached chains and failing brakes. The journey between home and school was about three miles over the hilliest terrain south of the Himalayas. I was frequently late for school, arriving puffing and anxious, and facing the prospect of having to telephone Helen after school and ask her to collect me. She particularly didn't like having to do so, and I knew she suspected I sabotaged the damned machine so as to avoid the pedalled struggle home. That bicycle was a beast and I've never trusted one since.

The day we broke up for the holidays was a casual day at Delamere, mostly spent tidying our desks and lockers. The deputy head announced at morning assembly that in the afternoon we were free to do whatever we wished. After lunch I climbed onto the hated bike and pedalled like a demon up the dreadful hill with, for once, a light heart.

At the stables I ran from box to box, peering in, until I found Cinderella where she stood in a darkened corner, recovering from her long journey. I rushed up to fling my arms around her. She cow-kicked, bit me on the upper arm and bolted out of the stable, the door of which I hadn't closed. With her tail held high, whinnying as she went, she galloped down a path, leapt a gate into a field of lucerne grass and started eating as if her life depended upon it. Waving a rope, weeping with pain and the fear of never seeing her again, I bopped up and down through the rows of grass, until I succeeded in catching her. She came happily enough, trails of greenery dangling from her mouth. I led her through the gate she had hurdled, straight into the crossed arms and clamped lips of the deputy head mistress.

She was a woman without mercy, and obviously no appreciation of horseflesh. She didn't give Cinderella a glance. I was to lock that animal back into its stable and get in the car. She drove me back to school, and prodded me into the Headmistress' office, where I was instantly expelled for leaving the school grounds without permission.

In my heart I knew I had done wrong. I knew I should not have left the premises. I was a wicked, disobedient girl. I hung my head in shame and fear. And I was expelled.

There are no words to adequately describe my misery. Despite my very best intentions, I'd messed up. There was no doubt in my mind that the pony I'd owned for less than an hour would be retracing her journey to Kajiado just as soon as my father learned of my disgrace. I seldom wept or let anybody see that I was wounded, but standing in the office at the school and listening to the woman's harsh voice,

119

and seeing my lovely pony dissolving before my eyes, scalding tears streamed down my face and neck, my nose streamed in sympathy, and I sobbed and really wanted to die. As soon as I could I would get back to the stables and slash my wrists, and die bloodily on the straw, my horse the last thing I would ever see.

There was a funny old character at the school, a kindly lady named Miss Baker-Beale. She wore her straight grey hair cut in a long fringe down to her eyes, and straight down the back of her neck to her slightly stooped shoulders, giving her a witch-like appearance that was quite inappropriate, because she was gentleness personified. She taught shorthand, typing and book-keeping, subjects that, together with home economics, were reserved for the stream of girls considered insufficiently bright to ever have 'proper careers'. Probably because I could keep my head above water in French and English I had scraped into the academic stream. I don't think I'd ever spoken to Miss Baker-Beale, but for some reason I shall never know she took up arms in my defence, and pleaded my case quite passionately. She was surprisingly forceful for somebody who was normally extremely timid. With slight reluctance the Headmistress reversed the expulsion, but under threat of just one more mistake and...

A condemned man given a 59th minute reprieve couldn't have felt more relieved. Happily abandoning the idea of the gorily romantic end I had planned, I got a lift back to the stables with a friend.

Every minute of my waking hours was spent at the stables that belonged, with the surrounding land and a palatial house at the end of Riverside Drive, to Sir Derek Erskine. Eton-educated, an ex-Guardsman and a member of Kenya's Legislative Council, he was the founder of the Kenya Amateur Athletics Association. He had made his money in Kenya from his grocery business, which had developed into a considerable empire. One of the few whites to embrace and support the African struggle for Independence, and a personal friend of Jomo Kenyatta, he'd made enemies amongst the white population who didn't support his views, and he was often lampooned. A tall, thin, greying, slightly stooped figure with a straggly moustache and a mild and quaint speech impediment that meant he pronounced his 'r's' as 'w's' – so he would call himself Dewick – he was enormously and discreetly generous. Derek took a particular interest in furthering the careers of promising Kenyan athletes, amongst them Kipchoge Keino, a young Nandi tribesman with fast feet, who would shortly become known as Kenya's greatest athlete. Sir Derek established the Kenya Amateur Athletics Association in 1950, and was its president for the next fifteen years. He also circumspectly provided financial assistance to a number of English families in Nairobi who had for one reason or another fallen on hard times. He was the personification of dignity and courtesy, as polite and considerate to his African servants as he was to the elite and powerful people who visited his house. In his top hat and pink hunting jacket he epitomised the English gentleman, with just the right hint of eccentricity.

The Erskine's house was a sensation to see, with a chequered black and white Italian marble entrance hall opening into a giant living room with a grand circular fireplace in the centre, overlooked by a minstrel's gallery to the first floor where the bedrooms were. There was an upstairs swimming pool, reached via Sir Derek's dressing room. The pool was glass-bottomed to allow people taking tea on the veranda below a worm's eye view of the swimmers. His two pet ostriches, Gert and Daisy free-ranged all over the grounds, and would obligingly swallow whole bricks and rocks so that we could watch these items spiralling from beak to belly via the long grey necks. Horses being what they are, although they passed these birds at least once every day, they never lost their fear of them. Many times I was carted home or catapulted to the ground by Cinderella having one of her panic attacks if Gert and Daisy were in sight, particularly if they decided to demonstrate one of their wing-flapping dances. They caused a stir the day they high-tailed it into Nairobi, creating merry hell in the traffic before finally being cornered and captured in the foyer of one of the local cinemas and driven home in a lorry.

Sir Derek's stables were almost as splendid as the house. Two rows of a dozen spacious brick-built loose boxes faced each other across cobbled pathways intersected with lawned areas, in the centre of which stood a three-tier octagonal stone fountain for the horses to drink from. At one end the rows of stables turned the corner towards each other beneath an archway surmounted by a great clock. Sir Derek's string of racehorses, polo ponies and hunters had their whims catered for by a fleet of African grooms, *syces*, under the sometimes tyrannical and usually irritable command of Captain Monty Archdale, a fiery little Irishman who suffered from diabetes. His blood sugar level could be measured by his prevailing temper: Jekyll one moment, Hyde the next. He and his wife Doris lived in one of the corners beneath the clock tower. Their kitchen was originally a stable; it led into a bedroom that in turn led to a small living room which was the twin of the tack room the other side of the entrance beneath the clock.

Despite 30 years of living in Kenya, Doris had only absorbed the very basic rudiments of the local language, and spoke an endearing mixture of pidgin-Swahili:

"Mary, can *wewe*[7] *kuja hapa*[8] and help me?" or

"Samuel, go and find *bwana*[9] and tell him *chakula's*[10] ready".

"If we don't get that *kuku*[11] in the *jiku* [12]soon, dinner will be very late."

She had invented a character called Mr. *Hapana Meme*[13], as a result of her servants always denying responsibility for anything broken or lost.

"Has *wewe* broken this plate, Mary?"

"No, Memsahib."

"Did you break the plate, Samuel?"

"No, Memsahib."

"Hmph. It must have been Mr. *Hapana Meme*, then."

Her passions were her dogs, good Yorkshire cooking – her quest was to produce the perfect oat cake – and a scattered wilderness where she strove against nature to replicate an English country garden. Beneath a floppy perm her face was dough-like, soft and shapeless, the same as Granny's. Invariably she wore a large straw hat and amorphous cotton frocks in floral prints as she meandered around her garden with her two ancient dogs shuffling around her feet. She was a kindly soul, and spent hours teaching me to cook the perfect pork pie and the lightest sponges, interrupted by experiments to have another go at the oat cakes. Her volcanic-tempered spouse was short and ramrod straight, with a bristly moustache and red cheeks. A permanent cigarette rode on his lower lip. He always wore a dapper little dog-tooth check hat, corduroy trousers and Tattersall shirt, the whole set off with his old regimental tie from the Enniskillen Dragoon Guards.

His equine charges, for whose training and maintenance he was responsible were a highly spirited and capricious bunch, prone to shooting off like arrows from a bow, or spinning around like tops. Sometimes for variety they might choose to lie down in a river, try to dislodge their riders by rubbing against a wall or tree, or hurl themselves over backwards; one polo pony named Gherkin once took off with her rider and hurdled a car that was passing on the road. The African *syces* who cared for and exercised them were naturally relaxed on even the most peppery mount. They slouched in the saddle like drunks, elbows akimbo, reins dangling limply, knees flapping in the wind, bare toes pointing to the ground, a very far cry from the tight military seat I had been taught by Major Blackwell. The horses adopted their laid-back attitude, and I can't recall seeing any of the *syces* ever parting company from their mounts, whereas it was something of a frequent occurrence for me.

There were a couple of other schoolgirls with horses at livery, but I preferred to ride out with the Africans, jogging along through the thick red dust into the areas known as the 'reserves', desolate neighbourhoods on the far outskirts of town where the natives lived in circular huts of mud and sticks with grass roofs. Their children and animals scrabbled around in the barren earth; the Kikuyu women were shaven-headed and their feet bare and flat. They wore at most a length of brightly patterned cloth around their bodies and huge beaded earrings that stretched their earlobes almost to their shoulders. Beneath the weight of the loads of logs they carried with leather thongs supported by their foreheads, they were bent over like question marks. But when they had 5-gallon tin drums filled with water balanced on their heads, they walked upright with seemingly effortless ease, conversing as they ambled along in a series of melodic grunts:

"*Aiee.*"

"*O.*"

"*Uwey*," which elicited similar replies that were incomprehensible to anybody else. The esteem in which a Kikuyu husband held his spouse could be judged by the thickness of her leather wood-carrying straps. The thicker the strap, the heavier load the woman could carry, and the more her husband would consequently love her. The women's bald heads were permanently grooved from the pressure of these tributes.

As we rode through the villages pot-bellied black children ran behind the horses, calling "*Nimwega!*[14]" smiling shyly and laughing, and scabby dogs snapped at the horses' heels. There was in these settlements a pervading air of ruefully resigned hopelessness. It seemed as if the people who lived there accepted their poverty with equanimity and made the best of what little they did have.

The *syce* who looked after Cinderella was a merry and gentle Kipsigis tribesman called Arap Rono. I enjoyed riding out with him, watching him cleaning saddlery, watching him grooming; in fact I enjoyed being with him because he was so relaxed and cheerful. Our conversations were limited to enquiring after each other's health, and remarking on the weather, but in his company I felt I was with a friend. I thought what a pity it was that he was black, otherwise maybe we could have been married in a simple ceremony on the lawn.

Every racehorse at the Riverside Drive stables had a 2-hour exercise each morning, mostly at the walk, up and down hills, to get them into perfect fitness, with a weekly visit to the racecourse for training gallops. These creatures lived a life of enviable luxury. Their round metal feeding bowls, called *kerais*, were personally filled by Captain Archdale from an aromatic vat of bubbling boiled barley and glutinous linseed, with added scoops of oats and bran, and cascades of thick black molasses, making a deliciously fragrant mixture quite good enough for 14-year-old girls to enjoy. As race day neared, the racehorses' thrice-daily meals were supplemented with pints of Guinness and a dozen raw eggs apiece.

124

Captain Archdale regularly added a handful of Epsom salts to their meals to make the horses 'go'. The *syces* hated Epsom salt night, because it resulted in very messy stables the following day. They had to be watched with an eagle eye to make sure they didn't tip the entire meal away. The interiors of the spacious loose boxes were white-painted and hock-high with clean straw, and kept pristine. An ill-aimed discharge following the Epsom salts dose could lead to a whole wall, or maybe two or three walls, needing scrubbing and repainting, extra work for the *syces*.

During the school holidays I was at the stables by 8.30am, back home for a quick lunch, and then spent the remainder of the day sitting on a pile of straw in Cinderella's stable, reading Agatha Christie or Zane Grey, while she munched her way through a net of hay. Nothing in the world could have lured me away. Nowhere in the world was there a happier fourteen-year-old girl.

I loved Cinderella. I loved the smell of her breath when she'd eaten hay, and the smell of her flesh when she sweated. I loved the smell of her droppings in the straw. I loved the gentle way she took a mint from between my lips and rummaged for more in my pockets with her soft nose. I loved the way her ears pricked as soon as she saw me cycle into the yard, and the soft whickering noise she made to greet me. I loved the way she galloped out into the field when I turned her loose, her head and tail high in the air, whinnying her pleasure. I loved the way she would see me from a distance and race across the paddock whinnying, jerking to a halt inches before the gate. I loved her spirit, her enthusiasm, her bravery, her willingness, and the wisdom in her dark eyes. I loved the way she stood quietly dozing in the warm afternoons, one hind leg bent, while I sat and read on the straw in her stable.

Occasionally a shadow darkened the sky, because when you love something so much, the thought of losing it is intolerable. Try as hard as I could, it seemed all too often that I blundered into committing some transgression, or was suspected of having done so, and then the threats would come.

"If you're going to do that, we're going to have to get rid of the horse."

Driving in the car one day we hit a pothole, and my head crashed into window. "Bugger!" I yelled in shock and pain.

"If that's how your horsey friends are teaching you to speak, the horse will have to go."

We were all going to take a drive together somewhere (unusually), and as I went to get into the car, Helen said: "You're wearing face powder!"

I wasn't – there were probably few girls with as little interest in personal appearance than I was, and I hadn't ever considered using face powder. I didn't even own any. I still don't.

"I'm not."

"Don't *lie* to me! I can see you're wearing it. Go and wash it off!"

I wanted to defend myself, to make them believe me, but it wasn't worth the risk of the threat about the horse. Obediently I went and washed off the non-existent powder, and apologised. They'd got me pretty well under control.

The stables were at the far end of Riverside Drive, where the road tapered out into a rough footpath across the plains. All the local residents were wealthy professional white people, and I knew most of them, occasionally baby-sitting for them or stopping by so they could admire Cinderella. Like all our family friends, these people went out of their way to make a fuss of me, inviting me on outings, or to tea in the garden, or to the drive-in cinema, and I often used to wonder why. Years later I learned that they had felt sorry for me, a girl who seemed to spend all her time with a horse instead of with her family. I was quite taken aback, because that was such a blissfully happy period in my life. I didn't want anything more, and had no idea that people thought I was in need of sympathy. They had an excessively poor opinion of my stepmother, and a very little better one of my father.

But my father and Helen did take an interest in Cinderella. He tried to ride her one day, and reached the end of the lane when she decided to return home and brought him back laughing and wobbling to her fast trot. They were always supportive when we competed at Pony Club events and shows, and were pleased with my modest successes. My father took a photograph of me holding a cup we won. Cinderella is leaning over her stable door; I'm holding the cup to her with a handful of oats in it; the two little girls are standing watching. But part of the photograph is missing. Helen had cut herself out of it.

On Sundays I rode with the Limuru Drag Hunt. The *syces* hacked all the horses over on the Saturday to whatever farm was hosting the hunt, where both horse and mount were accommodated overnight. On the Sunday morning an African runner set off dragging a sack of stinky stuff to lay the trail for hounds. Captain Archdale would drive me to the meet, where our mounts were ready with their manes woven into perfect even plaits by the *syces* and their saddlery gleaming to match their coats.

Fortified by a stirrup cup or maybe two of port, the hunt set off for exhilarating runs over the green and undulating tea-growing countryside. The gentlemen in top hats and pink (scarlet) jackets, the rest either wearing black or dog-tooth check jackets, white shirts and a white stock, and velvet riding hats. I didn't own a jacket so I rode in my white school uniform shirt and tie with black lace-up shoes because I didn't have riding boots. The hunt followed a route chosen by our hosts for the pure enjoyment of the ride. Nothing was chased or killed. The runs led over rivers and across the plains, over hedges and occasional barbed wire fences, where somebody would hang their jacket over the top strand so that the horses could see it and jump clear. At the end of a couple of hours we'd return to where we had set off from. While the *syces* took the horses to dry off and roll away their sweat in giant sandpits, hunt members tucked into lavish curry buffets supplied by the hosts. Although the hunting fraternity has a reputation for elitism and snobbery, the Limuru Hunt were a friendly easy-going crowd, maintaining correct standards of dress and behaviour without appearing ridiculous.

Getting to grips with the etiquette of the hunting field was a steep learning curve. The dogs are hounds, and never 'the' hounds; they have sterns instead of tails, give tongue instead of barking, and are counted in couples, never singly. The dress-code is quite complicated and riddled with status. To understand what people are talking about you have to learn a whole new language. But we won't go into all that, I'll just mention the hunt buttons. For those who don't know, this is a set of usually silver buttons engraved with the insignia of the hunt. They are awarded by the Master of the Hunt after consultation with the other hunt servants, to those people felt to have supported the hunt enthusiastically and with dedication. To be awarded the buttons is a considerable accolade. You sew them onto your jacket and wear them with pride, although if you go to hunt with a different hunt, courtesy says you must first ask the Master of that hunt whether you may wear them or not. Hunting is as much about etiquette as it is about hunting.

My father disapproved very strongly of me hunting, even though I explained to him that we didn't hunt a prey, but a bag of innards scented with aniseed. He couldn't accept that, arguing that something had had to be killed to provide the innards in the first place, and he was immune to my counter-argument that these were a by-product of the meat market that he supported. Irish stew and Lancashire hotpot were two of Helen's specialities. With hindsight, I suppose he resented the fact that I was so comfortable with the hunting folk, where I was ill-at-ease at home.

In my second year of hunting, Doris was brimming with excitement one day as she had heard that I was to be offered the hunt buttons. This was remarkable as on every occasion I hunted I committed, unwillingly, the cardinal sin of overtaking the Master, overtaking hounds, overtaking absolutely everybody and everything in sight, actually. Because once Cinderella took off there was no stopping her. She was a 'me-first' character through and through, and it says much for the tolerance of the rest of the field that I wasn't reprimanded at least, or pronounced *huntspersona non grata* at worst. You were expected to be able to control your horse, which I patently could not during a hunt.

The bestowing of the buttons, however, never took place because I didn't have the necessary jacket to stitch them on, and my father was adamant that I wasn't going to have one. His decision was relayed to the hunt, and no more was mentioned about the buttons. It was his way of underlining his displeasure. I wasn't greatly disappointed because status symbols didn't have any more meaning to me then

128

than they do now. I'd met many titled people and wealthy people over the years and discovered that they were people just like any others. Having a word in front of their name or a huge bank balance didn't make them any different. Having a jacket with the buttons on wouldn't make me more or less of a rider. Just knowing I had been chosen for the distinction gave me sufficient satisfaction.

I didn't know for quite some time that you had to subscribe to the Hunt annually, or pay a 'cap' each time you hunted, and that Sir Derek had been paying my subscription and caps for two years. I only found that out by accident. That was the sort of person he was. Many people both black and white would never know they owed him gratitude. He was such a very kindly, thoughtful and generous man, but never wanted any recognition for all he did for others.

On the Saturdays when Cinderella was travelling to the hunt for the following day, I used to go into Nairobi with a group of friends. Our pleasure was to make a fool of people, which was easily done.

We might point up into the sky, shading our eyes with our hands and shouting:

"Look, there it is again!"

If we did this for long enough a crowd of people would gather and stare at the nothing. Once a sufficiently large crowd had gathered we'd slink off, with a ball of string ready for our next victims. When we found a suitably naïve individual standing outside a shop, we'd explain to them that we were doing an experiment for maths, and had to measure the building. Could they please hold the end of string for us for just one minute while we went around to the corner to take the measurement? Of course they could for dear little schoolgirls like us. Then all we had to do was find a similar victim on the other side of the building, spin the same story, and leave the two people clutching the string. We'd covertly watch them as they stood there. After a while they began to suspect all was not well, and tried to hand the string to some other unwary passer-by, or furtively tie it to a door-handle.

If there was a horror film at the cinema we'd sit in the back row, rolling pieces of silver paper into small balls and flicking them at the backs of unsuspecting necks, making their owners jump with fright.

Such fun! And really very innocent teenage games.

At the stables I'd met another girl of my age, Vivien. She kept her pony with an English family nearby. It didn't have Cindy's jumping ability, and Vivien didn't share my nerves at going to shows. Although once I was in the ring I was fine and Cindy would fly over the jumps, for two days beforehand my stomach was a heaving quivering mass. I invited Vivien to ride Cindy, and soon she was jumping her successfully. Vivien went on to become one of Kenya's top lady riders, both in the show jumping arena and on the racecourse, and is still one of my dearest friends.

Once the new school term began, when the bell signalled release at 4.00pm I was on my bike and pedalling as fast as I could, which wasn't always very fast up the long and very steep hill on the way home. A brief stop off at the house to change into my riding clothes which were kept in the garage – they weren't allowed indoors – and I rushed back to where I had left my heart the previous evening. How soon I reached the stables depended entirely on the behaviour of the despised bicycle, which frequently engineered mishaps delaying my arrival, whereupon I would kick it and hurl it to the ground, and once jumped on the wheel and bent the spokes.

For a while, life went along very pleasantly, with no atmospheres and no scenes over omelettes.

# Chapter Seventeen

# Mummy

As I took shape as a fifteen-year-old girl, I started to attract boys. Until now they'd been mates to hang around with in a group, but now they were seeking me out more seriously. One particularly unattractive young man would nowadays be regarded as a stalker. Wherever I was, there he would be. Each day when I returned home from school he was sitting drinking tea and eating biscuits on the chintz settee which had survived the years, while Helen and my father smiled and nodded coy signals of approbation at me.

When you think of the sort of suitor you just don't want, think of this one. He looked like the prototype of the mad professor, with a thin bony face of very shiny skin, rising via a sharp pointed nose to a steep and unnaturally lengthy forehead, which was topped by unpleasant hair that rode in tight little greasy waves all over his head. At the frontal hairline there gleamed, permanently, a glistening green line of some gunk (I think it was called Brilliantine) that he put on his hair, and which threatened to slide down the forehead onto the rest of his face. He made loud braying noises at every remark addressed to him, and when he opened his thin lips he displayed a set of nasty pointed teeth. He was round-shouldered with a caved-in chest. For weeks he was waiting for me either at home or at the stables, seemingly unaware that I had no interest in him or his conversation or the boxes of sweets he showered on me.

"Goodness me, that young man is certainly taken with you!" Helen said.

"But I don't like him," I replied.

Still he'd be sitting there braying when I came home from school, and followed me in his car as I cycled to the stables. I ignored him as I saddled Cinderella and rode out of the yard, leaving him calling after me that he would be back the following day. Maybe he would still be traipsing behind me if he hadn't one day offered a lighted cigarette to my horse. He seemed to think it was funny. The very last view I had of him, as I led Cinderella away to her stable, was a distinctive red hand-shaped mark on his bony face, and his mouth gaping as his mind assimilated the torrent of invective screeched at him.

There were others, always invited in, engaged in conversation, plied with cups of tea, and their virtues extolled. With hindsight perhaps my father and Helen just thought it would be nice for me to have a boyfriend, but at the time it seemed that they simply wanted to offload me.

Towards the end of 1962, my father asked:

"How would you like to go to England for a holiday?"

What a strange idea, I thought. Why would I want to? What would I do there? Then he really took my breath away. He said that it was time for me to get in touch with my mother, who had been living in England for a few years. I wondered how he knew, what contact he had with her.

After eight years of neither seeing her or hearing her mentioned, I'd come to believe that I'd never see Mummy again. The idea of meeting her was frightening. Would she like me, want me or would I see the same disappointment that I saw in my father's eyes?

But in mid-December I was on board a London-bound plane with her telephone number in my pocket, leaving Cinderella in the hands of Vivien, whom I knew would love and care for her as well as I.

I stayed with Auntie Veronica, from whom I learned with great glee that cousin Jennifer had assaulted her beastly father, and pinned him to the ground and held him by the ears and banged his head hard on the floor until her aunt and uncle pulled her off. I wondered what he'd done this time, but was confident that whatever it was, he thoroughly deserved it. Bravo, Jennifer!

When I was in bed one morning the telephone rang in the hall, and I heard Auntie Veronica chatting to somebody. She had a piercing voice and I couldn't help overhearing.

"She's very quiet. Doesn't say much. She's got a very small face, but you've never seen a girl with so much hair!"

Telephoning my mother was the strangest experience. When I heard her voice, my mouth dried up.

I said: "It's Susan."

"Hello, darling," she replied. "How are you?" Just as if we had never been apart.

"I'm in England."

"Will you have time to come and see us?" she asked.

How long should I go for, I wondered. She might not like me, and so I thought two days would be best.

That would be lovely, she replied. She couldn't wait to see me.

I was to take the train to St Albans, where her husband John of the flamboyant moustache would collect me.

Auntie Veronica came with me to the station and put me on the train. When I stepped down at St Albans John was waiting with a great hug.

"Well, just look how you've grown into a beautiful young lady! You look frozen." He took off his jacket and buttoned me into it. "Let's get you home and warm you up. Your Mum's dying to see you."

At the time they were running a popular pub on the A41 in Hertfordshire, The Bell at London Colney. I felt sick as the car stopped. What would Mummy think when she saw me with my small face and so much hair?

Mummy was as I remembered her: curvy, smiling and relaxed. There were none of the emotional scenes I had feared. She didn't make a fuss, just acted as if we'd seen each other the day before, and didn't mention my hair. We went upstairs to the living accommodation and she introduced her four dogs who were sprawled over the carpet in front of the fire. John arrived with a tray of coffee and biscuits, then excused himself, leaving us together.

It was strange how here I felt instantly comfortable and relaxed, as if I had at last found somewhere I belonged, as if Mummy had never left. Her young daughter was staying with relatives in the West

133

Country and would be returning tomorrow. She was very excited at the thought of meeting me. I tried to feel excited, too, but truthfully I wanted to have my mother to myself for the two days I was there with her. We talked about school and Cindy, with no mention of my father or Helen. She told me of her life with John in Port Elizabeth, South Africa and their decision to return to England.

That evening I sat in the pub lounge watching John and Mummy serving drinks and meals. It was a lively, noisy place full of laughter. Regulars introduced themselves and said how much they had heard about me and how they had looked forward to meeting me. We ate roast beef sandwiches for supper. Mid-evening Mummy and I went upstairs and sat by the fire. She kept the conversation light, neutral and cheerful, mainly discussing books we both enjoyed reading. She had just finished Nicholas Monsarrat's *The Cruel Sea.* "You MUST read it," she said. One of these days I will.

When I went to bed that night she sat holding my hand, telling me how very much she had missed me, how she thought of me every day, and how happy she was that we were together. Then she kissed me goodnight, just as she had done every night before she went away.

We set off next day early by train for the winter sales. It was the first time I'd ever been to central London, and it was pandemonium. We could barely move in the department stores. Mummy had a neat little trick, though. She worked her way through the masses using her umbrella to prod the person in front in the back of their calf. When they spun around angrily she apologised profusely, simultaneously weaving her way around her victim and moving one place further forward. Having no dress sense nor interest in fashion I was at a loss, but by the time we were back on the train I had shopping bags of new clothes and a pair of 2" heeled shoes, something I was not allowed at home.

When we returned, John said he had some bad news. Lynn, their daughter, would not be back because she was snowed in with her grandparents in Devon. The only way in and out of where they lived was by helicopter. I didn't share Mummy's disappointment. I'd have her to myself for a little longer. It was strange thinking of her being someone else's mother, just as my father was somebody else's father.

Sitting in the bar that night I watched all the male customers striving to be the sole object of Mummy's merry attention. Not far away was a mental hospital, and some of the residents either came to the pub for a drink or were employed to help. They all adored Mummy. One old man sat on a bar stool from opening to closing with a glass of lemonade, never taking his eyes from her. When she later moved over 100 miles away he arrived on her new doorstep with a bunch of flowers and a box of chocolates. He was the same gentleman who spent much of the day riding his bicycle the wrong way around the major roundabout next to which the pub stood.

Next morning the room was lit by a bright glow through the curtains. Yesterday's green world had been transformed into a landscape of unbroken whiteness; beneath a pale sun three feet of snow glistened as if studded with diamond dust. It was the start of the coldest winter for over 200 years.

After lunch on the third day John drove me back to Auntie Veronica's, swaddled in the fur coat Mummy had wrapped around me. Again there was no great display of emotion, just a long hug and a gentle kiss on my forehead. The broken link between us had been repaired, and now we were in contact we could build on and strengthen it. Mummy was in my life again. It felt as if a piece that had been missing inside me was back in place. As we drove away Mummy stood waving from the door, just as Nan had stood on the dock all those years ago.

I imagine that the A41, at that time the main road to London from the north must have been cleared of snow because I recall it being a straightforward journey. John parked outside Auntie Veronica's house and watched as I walked up the driveway and the door opened. I turned and waved and he smiled back, then drove away.

Auntie Veronica was not impressed by the coat, which she was going to have to post back to Mummy.

"It's not real fur," she said. I peeled a tiny portion of the lining away, to reveal the underside.

"Yes it is," I said. "Look."

135

She sniffed. "Anyway, people don't wear beaver lamb these days, it's very common," and she didn't mean common as in frequently found, she meant common as in vulgar. Poor Mummy, even after all those years she wasn't being given any quarter. At that time I don't think people gave any thought to how fur coats were made. I know that had Mummy. been alive now, she wouldn't have thought of wearing one.

Two days before I was due to return to Kenya, a telegram arrived. I knew it could only mean that something terrible had happened to Cinderella, and I was crying as I opened it.

It was from Vivien. It said: 'You are on same plane as Cliff Richard. Please get his autograph'.

I cut a photograph of him from a magazine and glued it into my autograph book.

Cliff and the Shadows were travelling on tour to Kenya. On the plane I thrust the book into his hands while he was queuing up for the lavatory. He was quiet, very shy and rather spotty and signed his photo without a word.

Vivien and her mother met me at Nairobi airport, amongst a crowd of screaming teenagers yelling and waving to Cliff. First stop, before returning to the place I called home, was to the stables to assure myself that Cinderella was still there, with a leg at each corner.

# Chapter Eighteen

## A Working Woman

It was my last year of school and I didn't know what I was going to do when I left.

There was no career guidance at school, so I was unaware that professions like marine biologists, archaeologists, forensic scientists, journalists or engineers existed for females. Had I known then, I would have continued higher education. As it was, I couldn't wait to leave school. The available choices for a career were limited to teaching, nursing, or taking a secretarial course as 'something to fall back on'. My father had suggested sending me to Porlock Vale to train as a riding instructor, but not long before Sir Derek had asked if I would teach one of Jomo Kenyatta's young daughters, 12-year-old Wambui to ride. She was very nervous, just as I had once been, and within half an hour I'd realised that I was temperamentally unsuited and far too impatient to teach. And in any case, it would mean leaving Cinderella if I went to England. The prospect of emptying bedpans or sticking tubes into peoples' orifices held no appeal. That left secretarial work. Useless as I was at most subjects, I hadn't been quite dim enough to qualify for Miss Baker-Beale's classes, so my father would have to pay for me to go to secretarial college.

In the meantime our strange, strained family life continued. I felt as if I was looking in at myself through a window, and not really there at all. My father seemed to become ever more subdued. Never an ebullient person, it was as if someone had changed his light-bulb from 100 watts to 40; he didn't seem to have much glow in him any more. The new baby girl kept them occupied, and I did my best to remain inconspicuous and inoffensive.

My father's long leave had come round again, and they were off to England for four months, during which time I would leave school and start the secretarial training course. I wouldn't be going with them, but I couldn't stay in the house alone, and would need transport to travel back and forwards to college when I started. Through school friends I met a lovely family of three unconventional Greek sisters and their slightly bonkers father, who lived in Riverside Drive quite close to the stables. They were happy to have me as a paying guest at my father's expense.

All single ladies in their mid-forties, they had dedicated themselves to caring for their father. Aggie was terminally ill but had a tremendous spirit and sense of humour. She and her two attractive sisters were devout Roman Catholics. They embroidered priestly garments and altar cloths, and washed and ironed the church linen. Aggie worked when she was well enough, and Anne and Theo both had full time jobs. At the same time they had to contend with their parent who did just about everything he could to embarrass them, most particularly walking through the main streets of Nairobi and urinating in public view. He was also given to buying large bottles of aspirins from chemists, and then writing scathing letters to the newspaper describing how many of the tablets were cracked, or that a bottle that should have contained 100 pills had only contained 98.

Life with the sisters was unpredictable and fun. They did row and scream at each other, they did bang doors from time to time, and they really did get frightfully exasperated by their Poppa. These small explosions though were of no importance and forgotten almost before they happened. I enjoyed living there. I still cycled to and from school and then to the stables, returning for dinner where Poppa's latest escapades were the topic of conversation.

I left school with pleasure and a Grade 1 for my English Language School Certificate, much to the incredulity of the teachers and the Headmistress who had wanted to expel me. I was told no student in Kenya had ever achieved such a high grade. From being a wicked, idle good-for-nothing I had brought some sort of glory to their school, and when I went to collect my certificate the teachers clustered around me, beaming, and said: "Well, who'd have thought it?" I'd become an unlikely heroine. I'd managed to do rather well in French, too, and Literature, and scrape through all other subjects, even art. I wrote to my father in England, and reminded him that he'd promised me £10 if I got a good pass. He paid up, proud of me at last.

With the £10 I bought the double bridle I had so badly wanted for Cinderella. Stripping it down I soaked it in Neatsfoot oil, and lovingly polished it until the leather was as soft a silk.

With my school career finished, I moved on to the Temple College in Government Road, Nairobi. One of the Greek sisters would drop me off in the morning, to spend seven hours a day thumping the clattering keys of an ancient Remington manual typewriter. The machine pinged to warn the approach of the end of a line, clunked when you depressed the shift key and swooshed as you heaved the carriage back to the beginning. All performed rhythmically to a music tape that went 'da dada da dada, da da da dum dum', the carriage return coinciding with the final 'dum'. We learnt the basics of filing, and Pitman's shorthand to transform spoken words into identifiable squiggles that could be in their turn converted into written words and typed back. I thoroughly enjoyed learning shorthand and practised it at home feverishly, looking forward to the day I'd be qualified to have a job and earn my keep and Cinderella's.

When the family returned from their four-month holiday, the break had done us all good. Helen was cheerful, happy to have seen all her relatives and show them her children. Because she was happy, Daddy was happy too. And so was I.

With a mother who loved me and a certificate to prove that I wasn't after all a poor student, I began to find my self-confidence. After nine months I could type error-free at the required 60 words per minute and take shorthand dictation at 120 words per minute and transcribe it back accurately. A brown slice of rough paper bearing a red seal and my name and achievements written in shaky italics was proof that I was first class material for a secretarial position.

The next day I was walking on air, working as the sole secretary for the local auctioneer/estate agents Muter and Oswald, for the princely salary of £45 a month. A fully trained career woman at 16 years old.

Being a secretary was more varied and more fun than I had anticipated. It was nothing like the vision I had of sitting with a poised pencil hovering over a neat pad on my knee. There was the reception desk to man and the switchboard to operate. Flower arranging in reception. Identifying strange and sometimes unidentifiable objects brought in for auction – once a trunk containing two hundred sets of gents' woollen combinations with rubber-buttoned flaps before and aft. Numbering the items, creating the auction catalogue, typing it onto a stencil, running off the catalogues on the Gestetner duplicating machine that had to be filled with viscous black gunge. When the surveyors went to evaluate properties for sale, I went with them to write down and later type up the details. My duties also included tidying the stationery cupboard, keeping an inventory and organising the office messenger, an African gentleman whose tasks ranged from taking and collecting the post to and from the post office and washing up the coffee cups, to running errands like buying sandwiches or collecting dry cleaning. He was a polite man, and on his first day came at about 10.30am and said that he would like to take a short walk. I said he could go walking during his lunch hour. Again he said that he wanted to take a short walk, and again I said that he would have to wait until lunchtime. With utmost embarrassment, he crossed his legs and bent his knees, saying:

"Please, *memsahib*, I can't wait until then. I need to urinate immediately."

He went to do so in a nearby alley. The office lavatory was reserved for white staff.

Working here was interesting in many ways, and a perk was that I could earmark any item up for auction and the auctioneer would knock it down quickly in my favour. Cinderella quickly acquired quantities of saddlery and I finally had a pair of riding boots. But after three months the novelty wore off, and I started a new and significantly better paid job working for the chief accountant of the local Peugeot concession in Nairobi. It wasn't so interesting, but it was more secretarial than skivvy.

I'd been working for five months and was contented with life. I had started to develop a social circle, to meet new people and collect a string of boyfriends. I don't know what the ratio of European males to European females was at the time, but it was certainly strongly weighted in favour of the females. You could collect a new boyfriend every day of the week without any effort. Having boyfriends meant that I was able to travel around and become less dependent on my father. Paying my keep and Cinderella's, learning my job, meeting new friends, and having the freedom to go out when I wanted to – life was good. The difficulties of the past were gone forever. Helen seemed relaxed, the little girls were happy, although they were both shy and always hid behind their mother's skirts. This was a new beginning.

# Chapter Nineteen

## Moving Out and On

I remember the Saturday lunchtime when my father and I had just come home for work, and he announced that there was an epidemic of intestinal worms, and we all had to take wormers. They were large, chalky white tablets to be chewed after our food. We dutifully chewed them. They weren't unpleasant, merely tasted slightly of mint. Then he started laughing. It was one of his little pranks. They were just mints. His humour was very gentle.

As I did every Saturday after lunch, I went up to my room to read for an hour until the afternoon heat had subsided before I cycled to the stables. The mints repeated once or twice, and I smiled remembering Daddy's joke.

The bedroom door was smashed open so hard it hit the wall and the windows rattled. Helen stood in the doorway, her normally grey complexion almost purple. She was shaking with fury.

"Do you know that your father is down there washing the dishes?" she screamed. But it was not a question, it was an accusation.

"No, I didn't know."

"Well, I'm telling you!"

"But why isn't the houseboy doing it?"

"Because he's *ill*! *I'm* having to do *everything*, or perhaps you didn't notice!"

I worked five and a half days a week, was out all Saturday afternoon and Sunday and generally out on Saturday evening as well. Half an hour earlier we'd all been laughing at the lunch table over the 'wormers'. Nobody had mentioned the house servant was ill, nobody had asked if I would do the washing up. I'd have been perfectly willing to do so. But in this family you were expected to *know* things without being told. The last thing anybody normally did was talk.

The question went through my mind: "Why didn't you just ask me to do the washing up? Why are you standing there screaming at me?"

The injustice hit me. The years of cold silent atmospheres, the awkward meal times, the awareness that something was wrong and that nobody would say what. The constant disapproval. I started to fight back.

"Then why aren't *you* doing it?" I shouted.

She was so red and shaking she looked as if she might combust. Her eyes bulged, the veins stood out on her forehead and her lips drew back over clenched teeth.

"Get out! Go on, get out! Get out of this house. Go and find some man to keep you, like your whore of a mother!" She jabbed a shaking hand towards the stairs. She'd totally lost control.

I got up from the bed where I had sat rooted. I put on my shoes and walked past where she stood rigid in the doorway.

"And it's about time somebody told you the truth about your..."

My father ran up the stairs. It was the first and only time I ever heard him shout. "Helen! Stop!"

"She needs to be told what..."

"Stop!" he yelled. "STOP!"

I walked past him and down the stairs, and out of the door and into the garage. I pushed my bike into the driveway, climbed on and went to the only place I knew – the stables. I felt sick, shaken, furiously angry, curious. Her words followed me. What did I need to know the truth about? What didn't I know that she wanted to tell me and that my father stopped her?

I was also strangely elated and excited. This was a turning point. I'd been shoved out of the nest and was ready to spread my wings. I was growing up.

At the stables I asked Doris Archdale if she could suggest somewhere I could live. She listened while I recounted Helen's outburst, and picked up the telephone. Fifteen minutes later I was

143

living in the Erskine's great house up the hill, with the upstairs swimming pool and the marble entrance hall. Sir Derek's wife, Elizabeth, installed me in what had once been the billiard room. Nobody made any big fuss; I was told to settle in and that dinner was served at 7.00pm.

Pretty pleased with myself at having found such a quick solution to my predicament, I trotted down the hill to the stables and sat on the straw explaining to Cinderella what had happened.

I recognised the sound of my father's car, and his white, drawn face appeared over the stable door.

"Come on Sue, I'm taking you home. If anybody's going to leave, it isn't going to be you."

He looked so battered and worn. My heart hurt for him, but it also sang, because he was showing that he cared about me.

"It's OK, Daddy, I'm fine here. I've got to move out one day anyway. I'd much rather stay here, but can you still take me to and from work, please?"

I couldn't cycle backwards and forwards to work, a distance of several miles through chaotic traffic. White people didn't. I was a secretary now.

He didn't need much convincing, poor man, with the difficult wife and two small girls at home. We agreed that I would stay where I was for the time being, and he would collect me in the morning and bring me back in the evening. He packed my clothes and brought them to the stables, and that was it. I'd left home.

The English families living around the stables scooped me beneath their wings. One day Doris pressed a roll of notes into my hand saying that somebody wanted me to buy myself a treat. She never told me whom I owed thanks to for that kindness.

Freed from the constraints of any authority and the need to watch my every move, I began to enjoy life as I had never done before.

Mealtimes at the Erskines' were slightly unorthodox. Sir Derek sat at the head of the long table, his wife Elizabeth at the other end. There were generally an assortment of guests in between. Generous, kindly, big-hearted man that he was, Sir Derek did have one or two little foibles at the dining table. The first was that he should be

144

served first, ahead of all the guests, ahead of his wife. Meals frequently started with a bowl of vegetable soup, enlivened by a sprinkling of the enchantingly, crazily-named *pili pili hoho* that lived in a bottle on the table. *Pili pili hoho* is vinegar with a hot red chilli in it. *Pili pili* is the Swahili name for a hot red pepper, but what a *hoho* is I don't know. It has a magical way of turning even the plainest soup into something rather exciting. If there were a large number of people dining, by the time the last person had been served his soup and had splashed some *pili pili hoho* into it, Sir Derek had finished his and the servant was clearing away the bowls, empty or not. Eating a meal therefore became a test of speed, increasing in difficulty according to how low down the serving scale you happened to be.

Sir Derek's second little quirk was the halva. He had a great passion for the rich, oily sesame sweetmeat wrapped in silver paper in a little carton. This treasure lived in the wine cellar, a locked room with a wrought-iron door next to the dining room. As soon as the dessert dishes had been removed Sir Derek rose, took a key from his pocket, unlocked the wine cellar, took the packet of halva, brought it to the table, sat down, cut himself a piece and ate it with obvious ecstasy while the other diners conversed politely amongst themselves. Then he folded the remainder lovingly back in the silver paper, back in the little carton, and put it back in the wine cellar which he locked.

Despite their wealth and her own charitable and caring nature, Elizabeth was extremely frugal. Her thrift led her to the grocery storeroom of their business, where she selected from those items unfit for public sale and consumption those that didn't look *too* unfit. If a tin was not on the point of imminent explosion but merely bulging politely, it was OK. Weevils in biscuits or flour were not a problem – you sifted them out of the flour, and shook them out of the biscuits. It was a fact that if you lived in Kenya finding ants in the sugar, fleas on your legs or ticks on your animals was something you accepted and dealt with.

On one memorable occasion Doris was catering at a hunter trials, and I was helping her. We served tea, coffee, hot dogs, hamburgers, sandwiches and Doris's heavenly home-made cakes and biscuits. Elizabeth had kindly donated a very large and slightly swollen tin of pâté de foie, which was opened by inserting a small metal lip on the tin into a long thin key. Doris slid the key over the lip and turned. With a loud sigh of relief the tin in her hands became a missile, leaping around the caravan, squirting ribbons of hissing, putrefying pâté in all directions, over the ceiling, the saucepans, the sandwiches, the bread rolls, the hot dog sausages, cups, herself, me, absolutely everywhere, and sizzling on the tea urn. The stench was quite horrible, the mess indescribable, and we sat down on the floor and laughed until tears streamed down our faces, mingling with the meaty slush.

Poor Sir Derek was frequently unwell, positively green from eating food that was bad. There were occasions where he was in bed for days on end, but as a practising Christian Scientist Elizabeth forbade any form of medical care, or medicine, even though Sir Derek did not share her religious beliefs. She would pray, and he would pray, and we would all pray for him to recover. There were times when it was many days before there was any response to our collective entreaties. He would reappear days later, thinner and greyer than before.

People say that everyone remembers what they were doing, and where they were, on November 22nd 1963. I do. I was in the billiard room tuning in the radio to Top of the Pops. Instead of the familiar theme music, a man was talking rather hysterically, I thought. I checked the channel and my watch. Then I began listening. The President of the United States, John F Kennedy, had been assassinated in Dallas. I listened for five minutes until I was certain , then ran into the main house. Nobody there had heard the news, and until they turned on the radio they were sure I was mistaken.

While millions around the world were in a state of disbelief for weeks, as a self-centred and horse-besotted teenager trying to make a life for myself, I'd lost interest in the story within a couple of days, and hoped that Top of the Pops would be back at its usual time the following week.

A little over three weeks from that historic day there was another date ringed in red on the calendar of everyone in Kenya. On 12<sup>th</sup> December, 1963 Kenya would cease to become a British colony and would become an independent nation after a mere 68 years of British rule. The country would now be called 'Kenya' with a short 'e', rather than the 'Keenya' we had always known it by.

Jomo Kenyatta was the new president, and many whites feared a bloodbath. Because of the role he was suspected of playing in the Mau Mau movement, Kenyatta had spent many years of brutal imprisonment and desert exile under the British. It was not unreasonable to expect that once he was in power revenge on the whites would be top of his agenda.

When Independence, which the Kenyan people called *Uhuru*, arrived, it was a time of great joy and celebration for the black Africans. For many whites, though, it was the end of their time there as the senior positions that they had occupied in Government organisations were Africanised. However there was no bloodshed. Kenyatta preached '*Harambe!*' – Let's work together to build the country. He turned out to be a very moderate and well-loved leader, and soon became known as the Father of the Nation. For the majority of us life remained unchanged for the time being.

Derek kept a fine string of racehorses, hunters and polo ponies. There were often times when people came to ride them for one reason or another and I'd be asked to accompany them on a hack and show them the local area.

A chirpy little Cockney turned up one day to ride out one of the racehorses and invited me to ride with him. He was a pleasant young man and remarked what a beautiful pony Cinderella was. His name was Buster, otherwise R F Parnell, one of the all-time great jockeys. Pat Eddery was another occasional visitor.

One day a couple of Sir Derek's friends turned up to ride. She was a very fit striking-looking woman, and he was huge. Minstrel, Sir Derek's bay hunter was the largest horse in the stables. Next to his intended rider he looked like My Little Pony. Rally driver Erik Carlsson was a giant, and when it was obvious that poor Minstrel's legs would give way with Erik aboard, he took himself away for a couple of hours while I hacked out with his wife. Pat Moss Carlsson, sister of Stirling Moss had been a successful show jumper, but was now concentrating on rally driving. "I miss horses," she said. "I had to choose between riding and driving. And for now, driving has won."

If you had anything to do with horses and riding in Kenya at that time, it followed that you would end up meeting famous people, because anybody who was anybody either hunted, raced, played polo or simply kept them for enjoyment. Through Elizabeth and Derek I met other great Kenya characters: glamorous blonde Beryl Markham aviatrix, racehorse owner and trainer and *femme fatale*, jockey Sonny Bompas who referred to his old friend Haile Selassie as 'Highly Delighted', and the legendary Hoppy Marshall, who planned to write his memoirs. Elizabeth had asked me if I'd be willing to take them down and transcribe them, which I was more than happy to do. Hoppy – named thus because he limped, had an extraordinary life. He seemed very old to me as he sat puffing his pipe and talking about his early days in Kenya. He described his arrival in Nairobi at the beginning of the century, when it was little more than a shanty town, and of epidemics of terrible diseases and how he had worked nursing and burying the dead. On his next visit, he said, he'd tell me about his time as Kenya's public hangman. But he became ill and never came back. That this extraordinary man's memoirs have never been written is a tragedy, because although small of stature he was very much larger than life and one of the great characters of colonial Kenya.

# Chapter Twenty

## Mary's Hall

I couldn't live in the billiard room forever. Elizabeth Erskine had connections with Mary's Hall, a refined ladies' hostel in Nairobi and she secured me a room there. A 20-minute walk through a pretty park took me to the office in the centre of town. I walked to work in the morning, and my father picked me up at lunchtime, dropped me at the hostel, and delivered me back to work after lunch. In the evenings, I walked back to the hostel again.

It was becoming a struggle to support Cinderella. Living at Mary's Hall was good value, but it wasn't cheap. For a little over half of my monthly salary, I had a clean modern room and three meals a day, seven days a week. Cinderella's livery bills took most of the rest, but the hostel was too far from the stables to reach by bicycle. She'd been my personal island for nearly three years, and life without her was unimaginable. I would never sell her. I accepted the offer of a farmer friend who lived 100 hundred miles away. He would take her and look after her until I could find a way to bring her back.

Since my visit to Mummy at the end of 1962 we had written to each other regularly. Even though she lived thousands of miles away, I felt we were once again close after the long years when she was not in my life. One day we would spend more time together and get to know each other properly.

I was working hard, enjoying a social life and gaining self-confidence. Most weekends I spent away with friends on their farms, exploring more of the beautiful country where I lived. Our family had never ventured far from Nairobi, except for a holiday in Mombasa or a visit to the local game park. My closest friend's parents lived on the fertile Kinangop in the White Highlands, prime farming country. Under British colonial rule this area had been the exclusive preserve of Europeans. They had a beautiful old house lovingly built by themselves when they first settled there forty years earlier. The walls were wood-panelled, the floors highly polished, logs burned in the great fireplace, and from the living room they looked out through French windows over hundreds of acres of unspoilt land. But they were preparing to leave, forced out by the Land Settlement scheme under which their property was compulsorily purchased.

A year after they left we drove back one weekend. The landscape was now dotted with small fields of withered maize. The rest was barren. The windows of the house had old sacks covering them. Goats and sheep wandered through the rooms over the old wooden floor. The doors and wood panelling had been burned. The staff who had lived there and worked for them for decades were now on their own and had to fend for themselves.

I couldn't afford to run a car, but some weekends a friend drove me to Eldoret to see Cinderella, who was living happily on the farm and now had a little chestnut foal I christened Chantilly, just because I liked the sound of the name.

Kenya's aristocracy had their Happy Valley, but we led a fairly riotous life too. Friday nights many of the young farmers came to Nairobi to let their hair down for the weekend, and when the navy was in port they knew where to come to have fun. One of the secretaries where I was working was the hostess with the mostest and it was a rare weekend when she wasn't rounding up young single girls to entertain the scores of young men she collected. At her house I had my first taste of being disgustingly drunk on brandy and ginger. I woke up lying on the floor with my legs draped over the back of the settee and the worst headache and nausea I had ever known. Ever since, I've been bemused by anybody deliberately setting out to get drunk. Not that I haven't done so a few times, but never on purpose!

Kenya was a popular film location, and some of the girls would get together and hang around the sets in the hope of being extras. The girl in the next room to me banged on my door one evening.

"Quick," she said. "Grab your toothbrush. I'm spending the night with Robert Mitchum. You're invited too!"

"No thanks. He's a bit old for me," I said.

She came back later next day looking smug.

"Did you have a good time?" I asked.

"The best – the very, very best," she replied with a wink.

With regular letters from Mummy, daily contact with my father, the knowledge that Cinderella was safe and happy, a steady, undemanding job, busy social life with a string of boyfriends and all my domestic needs taken care of, life couldn't have been better. I had no plans for the future other than bringing Cinderella back to Nairobi, but before that I'd have to save up for a car and learn to drive.

# Chapter Twenty-one

## Riverside

It had been two years since I had seen Helen, when quite unexpectedly my father asked whether I would go for tea one afternoon, I think it was one of the little girl's birthdays. Whether it was to please him, or weakness or good manners on my part, I accepted when I would sooner have not. I'd been so much happier and confident since I'd cycled away from the house in Riverside Drive.

However, the afternoon passed reasonably, Helen and I were strung as tightly as tennis rackets, but we both made an effort to be light-hearted until it was time for me to go back to Mary's Hall for dinner.

Then they dropped a bombshell. They asked me to move back home. It was time to put the past behind us and live together properly like a family. I should have done what my head and heart urged, and said "No. Let's see each other, let's be friends, but let me keep the life I've made for myself." Instead, feebly, with an uncomfortable feeling that I was making a serious mistake, I agreed. One advantage I could see was that being back in Riverside Drive I'd be close to the stables so I could bring Cinderella back. First, though, I'd learn to drive so that I could be fully independent. I started saving for a car.

The atmosphere at home was less chilly than previously, and Helen was trying hard to be pleasant. We succeeded in getting along very much better than we had done before, with me at work 5½ days each week, and usually out with one or other boyfriend for most of the weekend, so we didn't have a lot of opportunity to step on each other's toes.

I changed boyfriends as often as I changed jobs. Both were easy to do; there were plenty of available young men and jobs for good English secretaries. Typing balance sheets, profit and loss and depreciation accounts for the Chief Accountant had lost its appeal. They had to be typed on astonishingly wide paper on an astonishingly wide typewriter carriage, with four carbon copies, and the least error meant re-doing them all over again. I was bored and began job-hunting again. At IBM I lasted four days because I couldn't get to grips with the proportional spacing golf ball and was asked to leave.

The mother of one of my friends ran an employment agency, and she contacted me to say there was an opportunity that might suit me, working for a senior Kenyan politician. It carried a high salary and considerable prestige. I went for an interview with his personal assistant, a pretty red-haired woman. After we'd talked for a while, she lent towards me, took my hand said: "You have excellent qualifications, but I think you are rather too young for this."

"But I'm 18," I said.

"You see, dear, the Minister travels a lot, and you would have to go with him."

"I don't mind travelling. I'd like it."

"He would expect you to share his bed," she said quietly. "It goes with the job. Would you be prepared to do that?"

She was right – I was far too young and far too naïve.

The politician, who had been regarded as a possible future president, was assassinated a few years later.

Instead I went to work for East African Breweries at Ruaraka, north of Nairobi. Each morning a chauffeur-driven car collected me from home and delivered me to the brewery, where I was one of only two females in an otherwise all-male environment. Most of the men at the brewery were fatherly figures who made a great fuss of me and vied with each other to be my daily favourite. The surest way to my heart was through chocolate, and Quality Control, Chief Brewer and Chief Engineer brought me bags full of every kind of chocolate bar available. I could easily munch my way through eight or ten bars

153

a day, without putting on an ounce of weight over my regular six-and-a-half stone. Why can't I do that today? Isn't life cruel?

The brewery produced a variety of lagers including White Cap, Allsops and their flagship Tusker, named, rather magnanimously I think, in honour of the original founder of the brewery, George Hurst, who was killed by an elephant. A perk of the job was a crate of beer every week, which was more of a bonus for my father than myself, as I couldn't stand the stuff.

It was a pleasant job, not terribly interesting in itself but there was a swimming pool for the use of staff and I spent most lunchtimes there with the other female secretary. There was an Italian mechanic working at the brewery. Although he was very shy, he was also very persistent and seemed to be wherever I went. Whatever I was doing, wherever I was sitting, there he was, polite, helpful, there, always, ever, continually there. By sheer relentless tenacity, he eventually persuaded me to go out with him.

One of my better characteristics was that I would never deliberately hurt or offend anybody if I could help it. This often meant that I ended up going out with people I didn't really want to. Tony was not the archetypical handsome Italian. He was very short and very broad, with a pleasant face. Had he been drop-dead gorgeous then rebuffing him would have been easy. But Tony's vulnerability made me anxious not to hurt his feelings. There was absolutely nothing in common between us but I couldn't shake him off, he just kept being where I was all the time and I found myself going out with him fairly regularly because I was worn down by his invitations. Helen and my father thought he was a marvellous find.

I'd been living back in Riverside Drive for three months. Coming home from work one evening I had only just stepped out of the company car when Helen met me at the front door. She was aglow with excitement. It was the very first and only time she ever seemed really, happily animated. Her cheeks and neck were flushed pink, and her grey eyes, usually cold and flat, were amazingly bright.

"We're leaving Kenya!"

"Oh. Where are you going to?"

"Helsinki!"

Helsinki. In Finland.

"When?"

"In three months

Since Independence, African children had started attending the school the two little girls went to. Not only did Helen and my father fear that academic standards would be lowered, they feared too that the girls might get lice, or scabies, or pick up any number of diseases or parasites. They had decided it was time to leave Kenya. They weren't the only ones – many whites at that time didn't see any long term future in Kenya, and were looking for new pastures – South Africa, New Zealand and Australia were the favoured destinations. Few who had enjoyed the relaxed spacious life in Kenya could contemplate returning to England, but I don't think there was another family moving to Finland.

"The best thing for you will be to go back to England," she continued.

I don't remember feeling any great sadness that they were leaving. I had always been an outsider. There was no question of me going with them to Finland even if I had wanted to. I wouldn't be allowed to work there under Finnish immigration laws. I had built a life for myself where I was happy and independent. I had a good job, plenty of friends and Kenya was my home. I knew nothing of life in England. I could not turn up on my mother's doorstep expecting shelter. Recently she had written that they were having a difficult time. John was working as a travelling salesman for Moussec sparkling wine, and she had taken a job as an office assistant. Granny had died some years ago, something I only found out in passing as nobody had mentioned it at the time. I hadn't forgotten my school friend telling me that Auntie Veronica wouldn't have me, so that wasn't an option.

And there was still Cinderella. Although she was living far away, one day I was going to have her back. She was my nucleus. I was going to stay in Kenya, come what may, and by any means I could devise.

So when I first heard the news it didn't greatly affect me. I'd move back to Mary's Hall and take up the life where I'd left off three months previously, learn to drive and buy a car, and get on with life. I wrote to ask if I could have my room back.

# Chapter Twenty-two

# A Rock and a Hard Place

Accommodation at Mary's Hall was at a premium. Elizabeth had used her influence to procure a place for me originally, but when I had given it up to go and live back at home somebody else had taken it. There were no vacancies, and a long waiting list.

My friend's mother had contacted me again with what she described as a once-in-a-lifetime job opportunity, and I had given notice at the brewery to start a new job in Nairobi town. I couldn't afford to rent a flat in town, but wouldn't be able to get to work without transport. So living in town was impossible, and so was living out of town unless I risked my life on a public transport bus. Even if I wasn't killed through reckless driving or wheels falling off from poor maintenance, it was simply not an acceptable way to travel. I could hardly arrive at work covered in chicken shit, or stinking of goat, or any of the other odours that were a fundamental ingredient in the ambience of local buses. Most of the passengers would have had little opportunity for advanced hygiene, living without running water and probably unable to afford soap, and they'd have to walk long distances to catch the bus. Had I been able to move back to the hostel it would not have been a problem. Now it was. Moving back home had torpedoed my new life.

The house was sold and the furniture packed up. Time was ticking away. I couldn't find anywhere to live that I could afford. That was the problem.

The solution came to me in a blinding flash of clarity. I'd get married.

Since I was sixteen I had had a relationship with a man who would have been the perfect husband. He was 'old Kenya', a farmer, horse-lover and in every way a gentleman; Eton educated, a decorated army officer, the leader of one of the pseudo-gangs who had infiltrated and destroyed Mau Mau groups. The pseudo-gangs were made up of extraordinarily brave men, the majority loyal black Africans and sometimes captured Mau Mau who had changed allegiance, as well as whites who disguised themselves as Mau Mau. They lived in the forests like the Mau Mau did. Eating, dressing, smelling and behaving correctly in every way to avoid detection. It was particularly dangerous for the whites who had to black up their skin and hair – the smallest speck of white skin or light-coloured hair could betray them. They dressed in clothing taken from Mau Mau prisoner and wigs made from their hair. To be captured by the Mau Mau would mean the most agonising death that could be invented by people notorious for their savagery.

When I left home at 16, while I considered myself self-sufficient and mature, the reality was that I was extremely naïve and could have found myself in all kinds of trouble. It was entirely thanks to the care and kindness of this man that I didn't. He taught me the ways of the world, how to behave, how to dress, and how to look after myself. He was ideal husband material, really. Except that he was 13 years older than me and divorced. Twice we had come close to getting engaged, but he had hesitated, saying that I was too young to tie myself down and it would be unfair. When I accepted that our time together was over I was heart-broken, but with the resilience of youth and an abundance of male companions to choose from, I was soon involved in a few innocent and frivolous friendships with young men who, like me, were simply looking to have a good time with no commitment. I knew, however, that with a minimum of encouragement any of them would have married me.

One was a dairy farmer who lived on a vast estate in the middle of nowhere; his nearest neighbours were an hour's bumpy drive away over a track that during the rainy season was completely impassable. We saw each other for two or three days once a fortnight when he came into town to attend meetings of the Milk Marketing Board. I'd spent a few weekends on the farm and found the place too isolated

158

and knew that when inevitably he had to be away for any length of time, I'd be afraid.

I eliminated another unknowing candidate because he was just too attractive and I knew I wasn't, nor ever would be, the only name in his address book.

There was a rally driver, wild and funny but a noisy eater. He smacked his lips irritatingly after every mouthful. It was as much as I could do not to scream and I couldn't imagine putting up with that at every meal for decades to come. The misophonia I'd developed since those evenings listening to my father slurping his pipe and the dog licking its genitals made me intolerant of certain noises to the point of violence. It's a strange disorder, hard to explain how it feels, but the irritation it causes is almost physical and arouses uncontrollable anger. Every time we had a meal or drink together I wanted to slap his face. I was beginning to run out of prospects as well as time and started looking at every new male I met as a potential spouse. But two months before I was going to be homeless I made a decision. I'd marry the Italian mechanic from the brewery.

The arrogance and cynicism of this shocks me profoundly now. But at the time all I could think of was how to survive. Tony was a mechanic from a poor family and I knew he was infatuated with me. In return for providing me with the essential transport I needed to remain living in Kenya and being able to have my horse back, he would have a wife who was pretty, bright and earning a good income. Plenty of men would regard me as a catch. I would make him a wife to be proud of and he would think he was the very bees knees. He had no idea how lucky he was going to be! It wasn't difficult to get him to ask me to marry him.

When I introduced him to my father and Helen, my father didn't express any qualms about me marrying a barely-literate Italian mechanic. If he had any concerns about my plans he didn't mention them. In my heart I knew I was doing something very wrong and foolish, and I hoped my father would show some concern and talk me out of it and suggest another solution. But of course we didn't talk: we never had.

If it had been one of my half-sisters announcing their intention to

159

marry somebody they barely knew, from across a cultural and social chasm, my father and Helen would have put all their feet down very firmly. But they expressed nothing other than delight at the fact that I would very soon become somebody else's responsibility, or problem. They gave me an electric toaster and sailed away to Finland with a cheerful wave and promises to write regularly.

I found digs in odd places. Firstly in a dark and grim property catering for elderly whites who had fallen on hard times. The communal dining room was so dark you could barely see what you were eating. The bedrooms were simple boxes all in a row like railway carriages, and there was a house rule that no dry cleaning fluids were to be used by the residents. After a while I found a room a little further from town, in a house belonging to a sweet but strange old lady who wore layers of bright-coloured make-up. She was the widow of the suggestively-named Jimmy Riddell who had twice been mayor of Nairobi.

So I had a well-paid job, somewhere to live, transport and a fiancé. And I was increasingly aware that I'd got myself into a dire mess from which I couldn't see any way out.

# Chapter Twenty-three

## La Suocera

The Italian mamma is legendary, isn't she? Doting on her male children, her cherubs, her heroes, the lights of her life, princes, kings, emperors, beyond reproach or criticism, and far too good for any other woman. If you think that all the stories about *la suocera* are exaggerated in any way, think again. My future mother-in-law was the blueprint for all other Italian mothers-in-law.

She was short and wide, always immaculately dressed in neat skirts and elegant tops she crocheted herself, her hair beautifully set and tinted a flattering shade of bluey-grey; a very proud, straight-backed and genuinely decent woman whose sole wish was to care for her family the best way she possibly could.

Tony's father was a handsome and amiable man who only wanted to play cards with his friends, watch football and make wine, and be left alone to get on with doing those things. He'd been captured in Ethiopia during the war, and subsequently imprisoned in Kenya, leaving his wife and two little boys struggling for survival in the Po valley in Italy. His imprisonment was ultimately beneficial for the family, because once the war was over he brought them all to this country where living was easy and there was loads of food.

Mamma's poverty-stricken origins had taught her how to make the best of almost nothing, and she could with just a small handful of minced pork or a couple of chicken wings conjure up a meal for the Gods. And like the wives of all his cronies, she was glad to spend her life making sure that her husband was totally contented and that nothing interrupted his pursuit of simple pleasures.

When Tony introduced me proudly to his parents and brother, they were overwhelmingly hospitable. Mamma's cooking had, and still has, no equal, and her kitchen was a gastronomic Aladdin's cave crammed with visual, tactile and olfactory *objets d'art*. She had never bought ready-made pasta in her life. Almost her entire day was spent preparing fresh pasta. It hung over the backs of chairs in long festoons, cushions of ravioli and parcels of tortellini sat on trays on the beds; sheets of lasagne and tubes of cannelloni dried on more trays in the kitchen; wherever you looked in her spotless little apartment, there was silky pasta. Pans bubbling on the stove with morsels of meat, finely chopped garlic, celery, carrot and parsley, and a splash of Marsala gave off aromas heavenly beyond description. Nobody could walk into Mamma's house without being seduced by those wonderful fragrances.

When Mamma sent me the first invitation to dine with them she wanted to know which was my favourite Italian dish. I replied that it was cannelloni.

On that evening I was rather peeved and disappointed to see a vast platter of cold meats: salami, mortadella, prosciutto. It seemed very rude of Mamma to ask me what I would like, and serve something entirely different. Still, manners matter, and I ate my fill gratefully, drank Pappa's excellent wine – he made this in large quantities from boxes of sultanas – and sat with a mindless smile on my face listening to them all shouting in a language I couldn't understand.

Mamma pressed more of the cold meats on me. I was already bursting at the seams and declined, to her evident disappointment. Didn't I like the meat, asked Tony. No, it was quite delicious, but I'd had as much as I could eat, thank you. He relayed this to Mamma, who laughed and put another slice of salami and another one of mortadella on my plate. I somehow managed to chew and swallow it, heaving a sigh of relief that I had acquitted myself politely.

Out went the dishes to the little kitchen that was like a miniature food factory. Then Mamma bustled back in with a beaming smile and a heavy shallow dish of something that she set proudly in the centre of the table. The cannelloni had arrived. I stared in horror as she put three cannelloni onto my plate. They looked and smelt divine, but I felt sick. I managed to cram one into my fully-packed

162

stomach, and by rolling my eyes, smacking my lips and rubbing my stomach tried to signal how much I'd enjoyed it. Mamma clapped her hands with delight, saying "*Dai, dai, mangi, mangi!*" It means "Go on, eat, eat!"

No use in protesting I was full. How could I be? I'd hardly touched a mouthful, said Mamma. I forced another cannelloni down, and Mamma suggested that maybe I'd prefer a little risotto, or just some simple tagliatelli with garlic and parmesan, if I didn't like the cannelloni? I shoved the third cannelloni down, somehow held it in my stomach against all my body's objections, and expelled a final discreet moan. Thank God that was over.

Out went the dishes, and back came Mamma again, this time, unbelievably, with a huge platter heaped with pork cutlets, lamb chops, fried chicken.

"*Dai, mangi!*" she laughed, pushing the meat mountain at me. I wanted to cry. With a superhuman effort I stuffed a lamb chop onto the heaving heap in my stomach, and then firmly pushed my plate away.

"Mamma is very upset. She thinks you don't like her cooking," said Tony.

"Please tell Mamma that her cooking is the best I've ever tasted," I said truthfully. "But there's too much. I've never seen so much food. At home spaghetti was a complete meal."

He translated this. Mamma refused to believe it, convinced I hadn't enjoyed the food. Next time, she said, she'd make something different.

I ate dinner with them almost every evening, and these spreads were a terrible ordeal for many months.

Used to Helen's meals precisely calculated to satisfy the appetite and no more, my stomach was not sufficiently expandable to accommodate the vast meals typical of an Italian family. The huge antipasto was only the equivalent of an orchestra tuning up; mountains of risotto or pasta were nothing more than the overture to the main performance – heaps of meat and potatoes cooked in various succulent ways. Every meal in their house was the equivalent of an English Christmas dinner, and it was months before

I could do justice to Mamma's cooking, and not leave her looking sceptically at my unfinished plate. But with time, my capacity grew, and it's been a losing battle ever since to get it back to where it once was.

The contrast between my previous almost-silent and inhibited lifestyle and the noisy and unrestrained behaviour in Tony's house took a long time to get used to. They probably found me a rather miserable creature because I didn't shout and wave my arms about or break into operatic arias, which I would have quite liked to do had I known how. But instead I formed a small one-woman island of inanely grinning bewilderment, as a way of trying to appear to be enjoying myself in their ebullient midst.

Tony's affable brother was married to the spoilt daughter of a wealthy local Italian family. His mother-in-law was a doppelganger for Endora from the television programme Bewitched. Everybody knew her as Endora. She favoured flamboyant red hair, tiny suede miniskirts, thigh-length boots and bucketsful of heavy gold jewellery. Her plump, placid husband just smiled continually and made pots and pots of money for her to spend or give to her daughter.

At 29 Tony was still living at home with his mother and had never had to lift a finger for himself – Mamma wouldn't have allowed him to do so even if he'd wanted to. I think the family were quite pleased their infant had found himself a girlfriend, but I'm certain that they had never considered the possibility he might do anything as foolhardy as marrying an English girl.

Months passed, and there were no wedding plans. I was the secret fiancée. He dared not tell his mother because he knew she would be horrified. We'd bought a ring but I wasn't to wear it in public in case anybody saw it and reported to Mamma. I found this frustrating, and insulting. Had I been smarter I would have accepted the status quo and enjoyed the free transport until a better arrangement hove into site. But I was not nearly as clever as I thought, and I did, despite my faults, have some morals.

The engagement would have to be broken gently to the family. Not rushed. Let them get to know me first. They'd known me for a year

by now, how much longer did they need? The penny was dropping that my intended was terrified of his mother. Mamma didn't let him leave the house unless he was dressed to her entire satisfaction, with a jacket just in case it got cold. He was treated like a five-year-old child, and in many ways behaved like one, which was his easiest option: you didn't argue with Mamma. He was her *bambino*.

Reliant on Tony for transport I began to lose touch with my friends, and became increasingly absorbed into the Italian community in Nairobi. The younger generation were easy to get on with, although their emotional personalities took some getting used to. Even a conversation about a recipe or the weather sounded like a declaration of war, because they were so noisy and volatile and constantly waving their arms about. The elder generation were at best polite to me. Knowing my mother had left my father for another man had indelibly branded me a scarlet woman. English women did not make good wives. They were unreliable, untrustworthy, didn't care for children and couldn't cook or sew. While they were always pleasant to my face they criticised me behind my back. Tony implied that I was lucky he was brave and generous enough to defy the advice of his elders and forgive my appalling family history.

I was totally in disarray. My self-confidence was whittled away. I knew that marrying Tony would be a dreadful mistake – the Italian elders were absolutely right. Now I had a breathing space, somewhere to live, I could probably have found a more suitable husband. But as I had been enjoying the transport facility offered by Tony, even my limited sense of decency would not let him down, which was how I saw it. There was no-one else to blame for this situation that could only end in disaster. There was nobody I felt I could talk to, and I didn't want to be a nuisance to anybody. So I kept quiet and carried on.

Finally Tony summoned up the courage to tell Mamma he was going to marry the English girl. She clearly wasn't happy, but had the good grace to welcome me into the family.

One event sticks in mind and still makes me smile today. Some elderly and very wealthy friends of Mamma and Pappa did nothing to hide their dislike for me, purely based on knowing that my mother and father had been divorced ten years earlier. On the only two occasions we had met they had been particularly cold and hostile. They had given my future brother-in-law and his wife a deluxe refrigerator as a wedding present. Tony was certain they would give us one, too. But they took him aside and said that as his marriage would not last, they wouldn't be wasting money on a refrigerator. Instead they gave us a tablecloth. He was outraged.

Mamma and her friends organised the wedding. I could choose my dress, though. I spent almost an entire day stitching small, delicate satin and net bags filled with sugared almonds and tied with a ribbon for each guest, the Italian version of confetti. It reminded me unpleasantly of hated needlework lessons at school when I had had to sew dolls' clothes.

Two of Tony's football friends were married to English girls, both a little older than me, in their mid-twenties, each with children. We saw each other often and they would become good friends. Neither was happy in their marriage but they made the best of it for the sake of their children. They were philosophical about their situation. Life in Kenya was so easy. The climate in Nairobi was as near to perfect as you could wish for. The cost of living was negligible, houses were spacious with large grounds, and servants were easily affordable. Nairobi had superb restaurants, lively nightclubs, an excellent theatre; within half an hour's drive you could be at one of hundreds of unspoilt beauty spots. Both girls had uncomfortable relationships with their husbands' families, but were fortunate that those families lived in Italy, not Kenya. When I think back now about the hostility shown towards English wives by the Italians, I suppose with WWII only twenty years behind us, it was still a fresh wound for the older generation of Italians who had been humiliated as prisoners of war of the British, whilst for those in their twenties it was merely a historical fact.

In those days there was an abyss between English and Italians when it came to women's lib. While English girls were burning their bras, wearing hotpants and miniskirts and sharing the love, Italian wives were expected to conduct themselves with propriety, keep their knees and shoulders covered and do exactly what their husbands told them.

My other English friends didn't say much about my engagement, and the fact that they didn't was an indication in itself of how they felt. On the increasingly rare occasions Tony and I socialised with them, I saw the looks on their faces when he drank too much. A group of us went out to eat one evening. Tony picked up the plastic vinegar bottle and squeezed it onto his chips, laughing. "Look, doing wee wee!" In a 6-year-old child it might have been amusing, but he was a 29-year-old man. I felt ashamed and embarrassed, but at the same time oddly protective. He was an innocent, really, quite out of his depth and uncomfortable outside his own family and social circle.

Whenever I see a bee with pollen on its legs, it reminds me of my wedding day. Tony's sister-in-law did my make-up. She used Orlane beauty products, which she said were made from bee pollen. I don't think she meant it unkindly when she said: "I've never known anybody who looks so different with make-up. It can make you look quite pretty. Today I'll make you beautiful."

Tony's brother gave me away. As we drove to the church in July of 1966, the enormity of what I was about to do hit home.

"Stop the car. I can't do this. Please take me back. I don't want to get married."

He laughed. "Don't be silly! It's only nerves. It's too late now. You've had all the presents, everybody is waiting, we've spent a lot of money on this wedding. You'll be fine."

We were married in the Italian church in Nairobi. I had promised the priest my children would be baptised and raised as Catholics. As it was an agreement extracted under duress – if you didn't agree, he wouldn't marry you – did not feel obliged to honour it. My children would be free to choose their own religion.

Never before or since have I felt so alone as I walked towards the altar between the smiling faces of the eighty guests seated in the pews.

I felt sick in my stomach realising that this was the beginning of reaping what I had sown. But at least, I consoled myself, I did have a means of transport, and could bring Cinderella back, so it wasn't entirely in vain.

Tony's parents had paid for a honeymoon on one of the sumptuous Lloyd Triestino liners, from Mombasa to Cape Town. As we were boarding the ship, my new husband spotted an old acquaintance. He told me to find our cabin while he went for a drink. When he appeared many hours later he was sick in the wash basin.

The ship was luxurious and the food, which I was now better equipped to handle in huge quantities, exquisite. But locked away with nothing to do but watch the sea going by, with a man with whom I'd nothing in common and who seemed to spend most of the day and night drinking, I spent too much time brooding over the awful situation I'd created. To add to the chronic eczema that flared up on my hands whenever I was under stress, the hay fever that lasted for months and the misophonia, I became claustrophobic, panicking at my inability to move off the ship. I couldn't bear the cabin door to be closed, and woke most nights screaming and sweating, my heart flapping like a trapped bird. I was a mess!

Woken from an alcoholic coma, Tony would push me roughly and tell me to shut up before people started thinking he was ill-treating me. The best part of the honeymoon was when it was over and I could get back to Nairobi and fetch Cinderella.

# Chapter Twenty-four

## Quella la!

Just because her little boy was no longer living with her didn't mean Mamma had given up on him. Far from it – she kept a gimlet and disapproving eye on his new home.

We had an excellent house servant/cook, a permanently good-natured man called Mwiba, with a perpetual wide smile and willingness to please. He had been trained by an Italian family and could cook Italian food almost as well as Mamma, as well as traditional English and Indian meals. During her daily visits Mammy always smelt the pans, dipped a spoon in to taste a sauce, added a bit of this, a bit of that, said there wasn't enough salt, you should never put cloves in stew, interfered, criticised, complained, meddled. While I accepted that her intentions were good, that still didn't make it easy to tolerate her forays into my home. But I held my peace, and Mwiba nodded and smiled and said: "*Ndio, Memsahib[15]*", and continued to cook in his own way.

My father had never drunk more than a pint of beer a day, and more often than not he'd slide over the mouth of the bottle a gadget designed to keep the gas in, and save half for the next day. At some of the wild parties from when I was living independently in Nairobi I had seen people very drunk, and had been occasionally been so myself. But I had no idea that there were people who were drunk every day. My experience of falling-over, belligerent, word-slurring drunks had been limited to films. That was changing, though. Soon I discovered I'd married an alcoholic.

Although I'd seen Tony drink too much after football matches, it had never crossed my mind that it would be a regular daily event.

169

His closest friend was an evil but personable old reprobate who was drunk 24-hours a day, every day. His idea of entertaining was to reduce his guests to a state of alcoholic paralysis in the shortest possible time. Tony often worked near there, and most lunchtimes they spent drinking together. Twelve pints of beer was normal. In the evening he reeled home to proudly announce how many bottles he had got through on that particular day. How he didn't crash the car was a miracle. I wasn't impressed. I usually find drunks both boring and silly. Often during the night I'd hear him in the dining room talking to the cat, whom he didn't particularly like, to cover the noise of the bottles clinking against the glass as he topped himself up.

Like his parents he was a naïve and simple soul from a small rural village in Italy. The whole family were warm, kind, hardworking and decent people. Being brought up to believe it was a man's right to be waited on hand and foot and a woman's duty to accept her husband's behaviour without question, he should have married a compliant, happy-go-lucky Italian girl, all the things I wasn't. He was not a bad person.

Tony saw himself in the same radiant light as his mother saw him, and still had the mentality of a small child. He worked hard for long hours and when he wasn't working he was either playing football or drinking. I had not taken into account that as well as providing transport, some form of common interest was an essential ingredient in a spouse. If I wanted an intelligent lively discussion at home, Mwiba was a superior conversationalist.

Neither Mamma nor Pappa knew a word of English, so we communicated in Swahili. I was learning Italian by listening to conversations and taking lessons and I understood a great deal more than they realised. I wanted to speak it, but with my self-confidence at its lowest ebb I was too shy to try. When I hesitatingly spoke a few words their jubilation was so embarrassing that I retreated into my English shell.

From the pieces of conversation that I understood, I learned that I had a new name: '*Quella la*'. A pretty name with a slightly exotic ring to it. It was what they called me when they talked about me. '*Quella la*'. Translated into English it means 'That one'.

Tony left the brewery to work for a large motor agency, and benefited from company housing, a pleasant and spacious old bungalow with a corrugated iron roof that made a pleasing noise when the rain drummed on it.

I was already working in Nairobi at my new job. The fates had smiled the day my friend's mother had sent me for an interview for that 'once-in-a-lifetime opportunity'.

"It's a perfect job for you," she said. "This man can be very difficult and demanding, but he's also very generous. You'll have plenty of free time. All you have to do is stand up to him. He has a terrible temper and all his secretaries have left in tears. If you can hold your own, I think you'll find this is a tremendous opportunity. He might sound like an ogre, but he'll be good to you. Just don't ever cry."

Half an hour later I knocked on the door and faced the ogre.

And half an hour after that I was the personal assistant to a one-man show, a volatile, arrogant and charismatic man paying me a small fortune, the majority of which went directly to an anonymous bank account set up by him for me in Liechtenstein.

We soon learned to get along. When he shouted, I slammed the filing cabinet door so it rocked, or whacked the carriage return of the nice new Facit typewriter so hard it shot off and onto the floor. He would then disappear for half an hour and return bearing small tokens of apology – cream cakes, picture postcards or small trinkets, and the tantrums were forgotten. He expected to be given as good as he gave, and had no time for tears.

As he was German and conducted most of his business in German, a language I didn't speak or understand, I never would fully grasp exactly what the business did. However it involved him meeting high level African politicians and businessmen, and travelling abroad for about nine months of the year on a variety of different passports. When he was away, he said, I should go to the office, open the mail, check that there was nothing urgent to deal with, and then go and ride my horse or go home and relax. He didn't want me sitting around in the office with nothing to do.

It sounded too good to be true, but it wasn't. For nearly five years I had a dream job and built up a healthy bank account in a tax haven. More often than not I spent an hour in the office and the rest of the day enjoying myself. When the boss came back he expected me to be on call at any hour of the day or night for as long as was needed, and that was a small price and one I was more than willing to pay. He was more fairy godfather than employer.

My father wrote from Helsinki from time to time, describing their new life there and sending photos of the little girls playing in the snow. I thought he would be proud of my new job, but he hadn't forgiven the Germans for the war and didn't approve of me working for one.

Mummy was saving up to come and visit, and wrote how much she was looking forward to meeting Tony. It would take a while, she said, because they were difficult times and money was tight. But we could wait, there was no hurry. When I wrote I never mentioned Tony's drinking or the fact that I heartily wished I had not married him. As far as they knew I was quite happy.

Tony taught me to drive, and soon I had a licence. At that time as well as knowing the Highway Code, how to do a three-point turn and emergency stop, you needed a bottle of good whisky placed on the examiner's seat at the beginning of the test. That assured a pass.

My in-laws were cheerful people who got together with friends at the weekends for huge meals, or drove out to fish in Lake Naivasha, or in the streams on Mount Kenya. They liked to have a good time all the time, even if it did sometimes sound as if war was just about to break out. There was always music and wine, and Tony had a powerful tenor voice and was a skilful accordion player. These were happy occasions.

So I had a great job, a busy social life, my own car, four dogs, a cat, a house provided by Tony's employers, a wonderful house servant who ran my life smoothly, no money worries, and Cinderella was back. We collected her and her beautiful liver chestnut foal from my friend's farm and brought them back to a small livery yard at Langata, in sight of the Ngong Hills.

I paid for her keep, our food, the servants, the electricity, water and telephone, and it never occurred to me to ask what Tony did with his money. I earned more than him, and had never had an interest in money for its own sake. It was just stuff you used to pay for the things you needed and wanted.

Chantilly had grown into a handsome two-year-old. I wasn't experienced enough to train her, so I offered her to some friends who had a tea farm. They were passionate horse lovers and would give her a wonderful home. One weekend they invited us to stay, to see how she was settling in. Jenny, our hostess, said their cook was making an Italian meal in Tony's honour. I'll always remember the sight of his face when the cook proudly placed a large dish of macaroni cheese on the table.

On the way home the following day, he said the food was disgusting. What was that horrible mess we had been given to eat?

It's one way of eating macaroni, I said, English people often eat it like that.

"Well, everybody knows that the English can't cook," he replied.

When we returned home he described it to Mamma, who shook her head in disbelief. Only the English could think of anything so horrible, she said. It was a truth universally accepted that English food was inedible.

For the first time in my life I began to cook, for pleasure not necessity, as Mwiba generally prepared all our meals. I bought the Robert Carrier magazine every month and tried out all his recipes, even boning and stuffing a whole chicken, which took some skill. I loved cooking, especially as I didn't have to do any of the washing up. But whatever I made Mamma didn't like, so after a while when they came to eat with us Mwiba prepared all the dishes. He didn't mind when she told him the béchamel needed more cheese, the pasta needed more salt, the pizza base was too thick or he should have put less celery in the sauce. "*Ndio, Memsahib*," he would smile.

Under the spell of Mamma's cooking my stomach expanded to accommodate ever larger portions of her *cibo squisito* – exquisite food. The very best Italian restaurant will never reach the standard she achieved in her little kitchen. She and I learned to rub along as I gradually started speaking Italian, and I recognised that her criticisms were meant to be helpful.

# Chapter Twenty-five

# The Blessing

Life was really far better than I deserved for that first year. Then my son was born.

Eight and a half months pregnant, I'd been suffering from severe back pain for several days. Ever since I had flown through the air off Jennifer at Machakos all those years ago, my back was never completely pain free, but this was something else and I had to call the doctor.

"How long have you had this pain?" he asked.

"About four days."

"It isn't back pain. It's labour," he said.

An hour later I was in hospital having a Caesarean section and when I woke I learned that I had a healthy son, but only thanks to the anaesthetist, Dr Mary Robertson-Glasgow. During the operation something had happened to my heart. My baby was born blue, and not breathing. The operating team had to concentrate on keeping me alive. As my doctor told me later, Dr Robertson-Glasgow said "Give me that baby," and she resuscitated him.

After his difficult start in life Rob was a happy and healthy baby. As most Europeans did I had hired an *ayah* – an African nurse – called Mary. Both she and Mwiba were besotted with Rob. When he was a month old I went back to work, knowing that when I came home I'd find him clean, fed and happy.

But Mamma, now also Nonna (Granny), wasn't happy. It was another truth universally accepted that English women didn't like children and had no idea how to look after them. She was satisfied with Mary, but worried what would happen to her grandson when I was looking after him.

On her daily visits, instead of prodding about in the saucepans, she marched straight into Rob's bedroom. First she closed the top window – I always left a few inches open for fresh air. Then she took the sleeping baby and fed him, over his vest and cosy pyjamas, into a little woolly bonnet and a thick woolly cardigan. She replaced him tenderly in the cot and covered him with an extra blanket. As he turned redder and redder and started to whimper, she picked him up and jiggled him about, reassuring him he was safe now Nonna was here. Nonna would look after him.

Laying him back into his cot she brushed her hands in satisfaction. "There! Now he's better. Nonna knows best." For a couple of days I watched, letting her enjoy her new grandchild. Then I said, nicely, that he was too hot, he slept better if he wasn't too wrapped up, and he needed fresh air in the bedroom.

"What do you know, you're English. You know nothing about being a mother. You didn't have a mother – she left you. I'll take care of my grandson."

One evening after I had watched her bustling around, I reversed the process. Opened the window. Stripped off the surplus blankets. Removed the bonnet, cardigan, extra vest, and said: "There. Now he's just the way I like him to be."

Mamma pursed her little rosebud lips and shouted, "That's right, go on, you'll soon kill him. Poor little soul, with such a careless mother."

Oh Solomon, where were you?

Rob was baptised at the Italian church, the first time I'd been back there since my wedding. There was a notice board on one wall, with a list of all the parishioners. Next to their names were the amounts they had donated to the church. Next to our name was zero.

One evening an Italian priest drove up to the house and came in with a small wand in his hand.

"*Buona sera, Signora,*" he said politely, then walked from room to room flicking the wand around and leaving small drops of water on the floor.

"I am blessing your house, *Signora*. The love of God be on you

176

and your son."

"Thank you," I replied.

"That will be one hundred shillings," he said.

Every evening Mamma/Nonna, handbag over her arm, upright, impeccably dressed and her blue rinse perfect arrived for two hours of tutting, advising and criticising. Every night Tony was drunk, falling over, falling out of bed and crashing onto the floor without interrupting his 100-decibel snores for a second.

I had everything I needed to break away. I had a car and was already paying all our living expenses. If I reduced the amount going into the Liechtenstein bank I could afford to rent somewhere to live. What held me back was knowing I would break Mamma/Nonna's heart, and that I owed this family something for the selfish way I had elbowed my way into their midst. Infuriating as Mamma/Nonna was, I was fond of her and knew that everything she said and did was with the best and kindest of intentions. It was as hard for her to accept my ways as it was for me to accept hers. In time we'd reach a compromise.

Mummy and I had written to each other regularly since we'd met four years earlier. She was thrilled to know she had a grandson, and was coming to stay that Christmas to meet my new family. I was longing to have her with me, to introduce her to Rob who would be five months old when she arrived.

In Kenya there was no postal delivery to the house – you rented a box at the post office and collected your mail from there. One Sunday evening two weeks before Mummy's arrival Tony went to the post office to check the mail box. He returned with a blue airmail letter from Nan.

I can see her handwriting today, and remember word for word what it said.

*'Dearest Susan, I fear I have very sad news. Mummy was knocked down by a car and badly injured. She never regained consciousness, and died on Monday. She was cremated today.'*

Today it may seem strange that Nan hadn't telephoned, but in 1967 phone calls between Kenya and England were very expensive. There were no personal computers, no Internet, no email. We only communicated in writing. What use would a telegram have been? Even more brutal than the letter. I stared and stared at the letter, thinking I must have misunderstood it, misread the meaning. It could not be true.

Tony said that he was sorry, telephoned his family to give them the news, and went to bed. I sat for a long time in the dark, thinking that if there was a God how much I hated him, and what a waste of one hundred shillings the blessing had been.

By the time the letter arrived Mummy had been dead for eight days.

Of all that had happened, and was still to happen, this hurt the most. Such a gaping feeling of loss. In the last fourteen years I had only spent two days with her. I felt such bitter resentment that I had never really known her, and that fate had decided I never would. All I had of her was a little marcasite brooch that John said I might have, and a lock of her hair from when she was a baby, which Nan gave me.

I wrote a list of everything that I knew about her:

She was merry and glamorous.

She adored animals.

She was slightly overweight.

She had a sweet tooth.

She'd lived in England, Kenya and South Africa.

She'd been married twice, and divorced once.

She'd had three children and lost one.

She had an American father.

She'd been coming home from work, stepped out from behind a bus, and was hit by a car.

That was all I could think of. It wasn't very much.

Within less than a year, her husband had married her best friend.

On Monday morning Tony went to work as usual without any mention of Mummy's death. I went to work too.

My boss was in the office.

"You don't look well," he said. "Are you ill?"

When I told him what had happened he put his arms around me and held me for a long time, and then went and bought a box of cream cakes and sent me home.

"Go and play with your baby, then go and ride your horse. Come back to work when you are ready. There's nothing here than can't wait." The ogre had a fluffy marshmallow heart.

I expected that in the evening Tony's family would come and offer their sympathy. They didn't. They never mentioned Mummy's death. It was as if it had not happened, or she was not deserving or important enough to worry about. I learned something from that, which is that when people suffer terrible losses they need to have an opportunity to talk about them. Being isolated with your sorrow is such a lonely place to be.

# Chapter Twenty-six

# Motherhood

As Rob grew, it became a universally accepted truth that I was an unfit mother. I left my son unwrapped in his cot with bare feet. I fed him unsuitable food. I had dogs and cats who would give him germs, and even worse, some terrapins. Didn't I know that a small boy in Italy had swallowed a terrapin whole, and had turned into a terrapin himself? That was the trouble with the English, they all hated children and had no idea how to care for them. Useless parents. More and more I began to doubt my ability as a mother. Maybe she was right. Maybe I was doing everything wrong.

And why did the English stand in a line when they were waiting to be served? Like stupid sheep. Rather a sheep than a pig, I snapped.

English food was very bad for children. It was bad for everyone. It was just bad, bad, bad. Children needed good Italian food – a nice plate of *pasta asciutta*, or *spaghettoni*. Mamma/Nonna told Rob he wouldn't grow if he ate English food. He should refuse to eat it. Which he did. He was a quick learner and dishes of food started splattering over the kitchen floor.

Despite the fact that she was the bane of my life, she and her husband doted on Rob and I tried not to show my frustration. Every weekend they asked to have him stay with them, so off he went on Friday evenings, returning Sunday night loaded with sweets and presents and admonishments to make sure he was properly fed, or to let Nonna know if he wasn't. Another week of gastronomic mutiny was in place.

One Sunday evening the grandparents arrived, and there was no sign of Rob.

"Now, don't get excited," said Mamma/Nonna as she bustled in to my house, handbag over arm, back ramrod straight as ever.

"Where is Rob?"

"He's safe in the car."

"Why is he in the car?"

"Because he's crying. Poor little boy, he doesn't want to come home. He wants to live with us."

I cannot describe my feelings of rage at this self-righteous, meddling little woman calmly telling me not to get excited because my son didn't want to come home, and expecting me to agree that he should go and live with them. No wonder he loved being with them, because every waking moment she devoted to spoiling him just as she had spoiled his father.

"Then I'm afraid he will have to stop visiting you, if he's going to cry when he has to come home. He won't be coming to you at the weekend any more."

She knew she had made a tactical *faux pas*, and snapped that now I could kill him, either deliberately or by my ignorance, stupid English girl that I was. I turned her round and fed her into their car and extracted a tearful Rob. For the next few months I kept him out of Mamma/Nonna's suffocating clutches. But getting him to eat what he was offered and convincing him that it didn't have to be Italian to be good was a long-term campaign. I felt certain that even at the age of three, his grandmother had instilled in him a lifelong suspicion that his mother wasn't quite up to the job. As little as he was he was quietly defiant and difficult and I was frustrated and angry.

Tony was not a tower of strength; as a matter of fact he was a tower of weakness. Mamma was Mamma, she knew best, I should listen to her. He didn't want me to upset her. Didn't I know how desperate she was to see her grandson?

I had learned that I was a piece in a matriarchal hierarchy. Of which I was the youngest and least significant member, whose opinions, feelings or emotions were of no consequence at all. If I stuck it out for long enough I too might one day reach the top of the pecking order and be able to make other hapless girls' lives misery.

It was crazy; the old lady adored the child but couldn't be satisfied unless she was taking over his soul. She had no understanding of, or interest in, the difficulty she was creating between him and me in our relationship.

After my mother's death, Nan came to stay. She loved the children, the country, the luxury of being waited on by the ever helpful Mwiba, the beautiful places we visited, and the meals we enjoyed with Mamma.

"My goodness, don't they eat a lot?" she said.

But she could see that my marriage was almost non-existent. On one hilarious occasion, during the night a drunken Tony staggered to the bathroom, and on his way back took the wrong door and tried to climb into bed with Nan. I heard him snarling "Get your bloody feet out of the way," and Nan responding, quite calmly, "Tony, it's Nan, you're in the wrong room."

Having Nan there helped to repair my self-confidence, knowing that there was somebody 'on my side', who didn't think I was a rotten mother, a hopeless housekeeper and an unsuitable wife (which, of course, I was).

We went on holiday to Italy to visit the family who lived in small villages in the Lombardy region. As we stepped off the train at Milan station where a cousin was coming to collect us, a crowd gathered around and pointed at me, murmuring and tutting.

"What are those people looking at?" I asked Tony.

"They are looking at you because you are dressed like a prostitute. Decent women don't wear miniskirts."

I looked down at my legs. My skirt was six inches above my knees, and by the standards of 1968 relatively conservative. It was far from being a pussy pelmet.

They wore mini-skirts in Kenya, they wore them in England and they wore them in France, but apparently in Italy mini-skirts were the sign of a loose woman.

Tony's relatives overwhelmed us with hospitality and generosity, but they were shocked by my clothes and couldn't believe that I didn't put shoes on Rob when he was in his pushchair. They were convinced he'd catch pneumonia, although it was the height of summer and 40 Centigrade degrees of heat beat off the pavements and walls of the towns and villages. We went from one family to another, eating and drinking, and I was examined like a strange insect, because these country people had never met an English person before. One aunt touched my skin to see if it felt the same as Italian skin, and a small boy burst into tears. He had expected me to be black. They lamented that I didn't eat enough, although I tried my best. They pinched my cheeks and paraded Rob around to show their friends and neighbours. They were proud that after their earlier poverty and the difficulties of surviving the war they now had modern comfortable houses. Suites of fancy furniture were covered in cellophane and kept in an unused room. The black and white televisions had a sheet of plastic taped over the front – blue at the top, pink in the middle and green at the bottom – to give a coloured effect.

They were warm-hearted and affectionate, nosy and critical, and gossiped about everybody. Net curtains were never still, as neighbour watched neighbour going about their daily business; they knew exactly what Signora next door had bought at the butcher, and how she would cook it. But as friendly as they were, I sometimes heard them talking when they couldn't see me, and what they said then was never very flattering.

Every meal was a banquet of heavenly delights – except for the cockerel's head. When our hostess put it on a plate in front of me I thought it was a joke. The sinewy neck, the tongue protruding from the gaping beak, the blind eyes, the comb and wattles lying there like a surreal still life painting. I laughed politely. All the guests watched, waiting for me to begin. *"Dai, mangi!"* they cried. I shook my head, still laughing politely.

"It's the best part," said Tony. "You have to eat it. It's an honour."

"I'm not eating it," I said. "Tell them whatever you like, but I'm not eating it."

One of his cousins, a handsome man sitting on my right who had been stroking my leg under the table took the plate from me, and gave me his which sported a more conventional chicken cut, a leg.

We spent six weeks touring glorious northern Italy. Milan, Verona, Venice, Mantua, Lake Garda and the Dolomites.

I liked Italians; I liked their language; I loved their music; I loved their food, I liked many of them individually. However, I found their culture archaic. In the evenings once they had eaten the men dressed in their finest and went to walk around the towns, looking at their reflections in shop windows, while their wives sat at home knitting, crocheting, ironing or making pasta for the next day.

In Kenya the younger wives were more liberated. They all went out to work and when their men were out enjoying themselves, so were they, somewhere else. And they all had their parents near by, something I envied.

The arrival of my daughter passed with less fanfare, as little girls didn't suffer the overwhelming adulation afforded to little Italian boys. Not that Mamma/Nonna and Pappa/Nonno didn't adore Julie – they did. But all their energy and concern was focused on Rob and whether or not he was being brought up as a proper little Italian boy deserved.

While Julie was being born her father was out drinking with his degenerate old friend, whose daughter he had been pursuing for many months. This suited me as it meant we spent very little time together. For Christmas that year he gave me a couple of pillow cases. He was sorry it was all he could afford, but he had spent all his money buying her a tape recorder.

He was infatuated with the girl. I hoped he would want to leave me and marry her, so that with a clear conscience I could have my life back in my own hands. But disappointingly he didn't show any signs of going off with her. I think he knew that Mamma/Nonna would have tolerated a half-caste daughter-in-law even less than an English one. Except when his parents were around, Tony paid almost no attention to the children. Only in their company was he the devoted father. There were occasional ructions with the in-laws. I didn't appreciate the casual kicks my father-in-law aimed at my dogs, and Mamma continued to meddle relentlessly, but she knew just how far she could push me and stayed on her side of the line.

Tony changed his job so we had to leave the company house. From my savings in Liechtenstein I bought a stone bungalow down a long jacaranda-lined drive, with a terraced garden leading down to a river and a grove of banana trees. Outside the kitchen were loquat and avocado trees; the hedges were woven with passion fruit vines. There were lawns for the children to run on, and shady trees for them to sleep beneath in the afternoon. The garden was a riot of colour from the thousands of impatiens flowers whose seed pods exploded when touched. We had chickens for our own eggs which we gave to friends and family. I offered them to the elderly wealthy people who had given us the tablecloth wedding present. When I next saw them, the wife said she had put them in a bowl of water to test them for freshness but they had floated so she'd thrown them away. She didn't want any more of our eggs. She had an obsession about germs and food poisoning, so she washed all salad and fruit in potassium permanganate. When she didn't have any, she used Dettol instead. I can't recommend that.

In most ways life was idyllic. I had two beautiful children, pets, a lovely house and garden, a fabulous job and Cinderella. But Kenya was going through a difficult period. There was political uncertainty, and threats of currency restrictions which would mean that if you sold your house and wanted to leave the country you could not take enough of your own money with you to start life elsewhere. I either could not or would not adapt to the Italian way of life and accept my mother-in-law's constant criticism and efforts to dominate me. Rob continued to be defiant and I felt I was losing him to her. After months of agonising soul-searching I decided to leave Kenya. I told Tony I was going to take the children and live in England. He could come with me, or stay. He decided to come with us.

Mamma threatened to die of a broken heart at the thought of being separated from her son and grandson. I was sympathetic in one way, and at the same time awed by her inability to think outside of her own need. How did she think I felt about leaving my horse and other pets?

The dogs and cats were rehomed and I entrusted Cinderella to the care of a friend who I knew would love and look after her for the rest of her life. Saying goodbye to her broke my heart. When we left Mwiba the house-servant and Mary the *ayah* wept at the airport, and the grandparents tried to put on a brave face. I was far sadder to leave the servants than the in-laws. They had been a part of the family, always cheerful, helpful, doting on the children, doing everything they could to ensure our lives ran smoothly. They were as much friends as employees, and I was going to miss them more than I can say.

# Chapter Twenty-seven

# Hertfordshire

A year previously my father and Helen had left Finland and were living in Hertfordshire, and that's where we decided to start looking for a home and work.

My father met us at the airport and delivered us directly to a motel into which he had booked us. Tony was mortally offended and I was embarrassed that they had not invited us to stay at least for a couple of days in their spacious house, or even for a meal when we arrived.

Tony quickly found a job as a workshop foreman, and I found us a rented flat.

It was not only the climate that we had to adapt to, it was a totally alien way of life. In Kenya Mwiba gave me a list each week of groceries, meat and vegetables. In the supermarket all I had to do was drop things in the trolley and put them on the conveyor. Someone packed them into cartons at the other end, and put them in the car. At home Mwiba unloaded and unpacked them and put them away. Shopping was easy. Then he transformed these things into meals, which he served, cleared away, washed up, and then put the crockery and cutlery away. Eating was easy.

It was a different game now. I unloaded trolleys of goods at the cash desk and stood gazing around the supermarket, while a mountain of jars, packets, boxes and rolls piled up at the other end under the impatient eye of the cashier and the growing queue shuffling behind me. All this stuff had to be packed into bags by me, carried to the car by me; unloaded and put away by me; it was a real drag. That was before I'd even started thinking what I was going to do with it. There was such a bewildering array of cleaning products:

stuff for ovens, stuff for windows, for carpets, for upholstery, for bathrooms, kitchens; washing up liquids and laundry powders; floor cleaners: how on earth was one supposed to choose? Shelf upon shelf of liquids, creams, sprays and powders. In Kenya Mwiba had used one product for cleaning everything. He cleaned our clothes, the floors, the washing up, the bathroom and the kitchen with Omo. I'd no idea at all where to begin; I'd never ironed, dusted, hoovered, gardened or washed dishes. I didn't know the difference between a spin drier and a tumble drier, a top-loader and a twin-tub. A challenging and perplexing new world was unfolding.

Rob came home from school in tears one afternoon.

The form teacher had asked each child its nationality, and he'd replied "African" to loud laughter and the teacher's explanation that he couldn't be African because he wasn't black. He was most upset. To cheer him up I suggested he should invite a friend home for tea next day, and laid on what I thought was a very fine spread. The day after he came home crying again.

"That boy said tea was rubbish at our house," he sobbed.

"Well, he certainly ate enough of it," I said, feeling rather indignant as our visitor had munched his way heartily through piles of sandwiches, cakes, biscuits, Angel Delight, chocolate bars and ice cream.

"But when boys have tea here," explained Rob, "they have sausages or burgers with chips and things."

"That's supper, not tea," I replied.

"Well," he said darkly "it's what they call tea in England."

I began house-hunting in the pleasant country town of St Albans. Used to spacious Kenyan houses and gardens it was a shock to find how little my Liechtenstein savings would buy in England. There would be no bungalow standing in landscaped gardens leading to a river. A few months later we moved into a small modern town house on the outskirts of St Albans. The front door blew open in a gust of wind and the handle embedded itself in the cardboard wall. There were other equally nasty houses each side, and to the back. We could hear the neighbours breathing. It was really quite horrible. After we'd lived in the new house for several months I noticed that the bath was discoloured and had developed a rough, scratchy texture. I mentioned to Helen that I'd have to buy a new one.

"What bath cleaner do you use?" she asked.

"Bath cleaner?"

I didn't know you had to clean them; I thought that the soapy water did the job automatically. Helen was less hostile now and she was very fond of the children. Her two daughters were growing up shy, introverted and gentle, and, like their mother, completely lacking in self-confidence. I visited them regularly and invited them around frequently. They were always pleasant in a slightly distant way. No more and no less. My father seemed very quiet. He puffed his pipe and pottered around. It was disconcerting that whenever we visited them nobody ever offered a cup of tea or a drink, and certainly we were never invited for a meal. It all felt rather odd.

My savings were not sufficient to pay outright for the house, so we would have to have a mortgage, and for that I had to find a job. My dream of being a stay-at-home mother was out of the window. I was confident that I'd have no difficulty finding a well-paid position, but was brought crashing down to reality at my first interview. A kindly gentleman complimented me on my experience and excellent references but explained that my children would contract mumps, measles, chicken pox, German measles, stomach upsets, whooping cough, sore throats, ear ache and a whole host of other ailments that would make me totally unsuited to any sort of regular employment. Everywhere I went it was the same. Mothers with young children did not make reliable secretaries.

Ironically, the only place who would employ me as, of all things, a machinist, was a local factory making quality ladies' coats for Aquascutum. They provided a crèche for employees' children during the school holidays. Just like at boarding school, I became a number – No. 291. Given my aversion to and ineptitude for any form of sewing it couldn't have been a more incongruous occupation, but it was the only place I could find that would have me. Each morning, after delivering Rob to school and Julie to a childminder, I arrived at the factory, punched a little card into a machine, and sat down to sew.

189

With the exception of a couple of men, the rest of the machinists were all ladies from the surrounding council estates. They frequently arrived at work with black eyes or split lips, accepting domestic violence as a normal part of married life. They were unfailingly bawdy and cheerful. The malevolent industrial sewing machines never missed an opportunity to skewer their thick, high-speed needles through slow fingers. We sat in rows in a decrepit dusty building, machining mile upon mile of precision stitches each day. Each stitch had to be an exact pre-defined length, and an exact pre-defined distance from the seam. The instructions were on little tickets pinned to the expensive pieces of cloth dumped in our baskets. A supervisor with a ruler walked around all day measuring distances and stitch lengths, and if they didn't conform perfectly you had to rip them all out and start again. That's what I spent most of my time doing.

Our working day was regulated by a series of bells and punching snips into our number cards. The mid-morning fifteen-minute tea break galvanised the entire workforce into scrambling up the stairs to the canteen to snatch a cup of stewed tea and a biscuit, with little time to savour it before the bell signalled that it was time to get back to business. There was a similar bell at lunchtime, when we punched a snip in our card before going to the canteen for lunch. Then you punched a further snip before resuming your post for the afternoon shift until the final bell released you to snip the card for the fourth and last time that day.

Each Friday part of our lunch break was spent waiting for a clerk to call our number to go to a little window and receive a small brown envelope containing our ridiculous wages. My father was appalled and angry that I was working in a factory, but as far as I was concerned it was simply a means to an end. I would have done pretty much anything to earn a living.

'Christmas Dinner' was rather special, because instead of queuing up at lunchtime with rubber mats on our hands to receive whatever plateful of hot food might be slapped upon it, we sat at the long tables which for the occasion had been laid with paper cloths. Senior staff, led by the floor manager, a courtly and charming gentleman, served the meal. Sliced rounds of tinned turkey, warm vegetables with gravy, and Christmas pudding with custard. The girls really looked forward to this event. They loved being waited on by 'old Bennett, and Mrs Toffee-nose', and groaned when the bell, dead on cue, yelled at us to snip our cards and get back to our benches.

The years had done nothing to increase my skills as a seamstress. Although I really did try very hard, there was no question that I was the most inept worker in the place. My task was to insert sleeves into the coat panels. There was no tacking or pinning. The fabric had to be pinched, teased and cajoled into place so that there were no folds or creases and all the notches aligned perfectly. The minimum target was six coats an hour. On a good day I might manage four, but more often than not I spent most of my time unpicking stitches that had strayed from the straight and narrow. Apart from the actual work, which I loathed, I quite enjoyed my time at the factory, and learned a great deal about life from my colleagues. We came from very different backgrounds, and they laughed at my 'posh' accent, but not unkindly. Some of them lived in awful circumstances, with men who beat them and kids who were uncontrollable, but they were always cheerful and passed most of the day calling out ribald remarks to each other or telling lewd jokes. So the year I spent there passed quickly, and did mean that I could bring home enough money to ensure that the mortgage was paid and we all had enough to eat.

The Personnel Manager, an acid woman, asked me one day if I knew why I was employed there. The idea, she explained, was to make money for the factory. In an unusual version of the employer/employee relationship, it was costing them to keep me there. Rather a mean thing to say, I felt, but true. I had learned to stitch a straight seam, and had started quite successfully making clothes for the children and myself. The problem was that I could not do it fast enough in the factory.

There was a world of difference between the price of a weekly shop in Kenya and that in England. Everything was far more expensive, especially meat, and Tony demanded steak daily, as well as the imperative pasta beforehand. He washed it all down with lavish quantities of whisky, and rounded off the evening with a nice fat cigar or two. Our standard of living fell sharply, with his income barely enough to cover the cost of the whisky and cigars, and mine stretched to take care of the other bills and mortgage. I don't know if he was happy in his new life; we talked so little and had no mutual interest. He didn't visit the children's school, nor go to any of the events there. He wasn't unkind to them, he just didn't want to entertain them. He was more of a child than a parent.

We'd been living in England for six months, when Tony's brother telephoned from Kenya one day when Tony was out. Normally mild and easy-going, he was furious.

"What the hell is this fucking bill all about?" he shouted.

"What bill? What are you talking about?" I asked.

"Six thousand shillings, your unpaid account at the store. They're asking me to pay it."

"I never had an account at any store," I replied. "I don't know anything about it. What store, and what is the bill for?"

"The Asian store near your house. And most of it's for alcohol."

"Then you'll have to speak to your brother and sort it out with him. You know I hardly ever drink alcohol. It's nothing to do with me."

"How could he have spent so much on drink?" he said.

"You'd better ask him."

As the months went by, Tony drank increasingly heavily, and became belligerent and hostile. When friends visited, he'd pour himself drink after drink, without offering any. If people came to eat with us, he'd remark that I was a hopeless cook. Soon nobody wanted to come to the house.

And, as I would subsequently learn, very much later, he had been telling people that I wasn't working in St Albans during the day. I was in London working as a prostitute.

# Chapter Twenty-eight

## Smoked Salmon and Lambrusco

The first major row with Helen erupted when I bought a couple of kittens and took them to show her. Far from being enchanted, she was absolutely furious.

"How dare you bring them here!" she shouted. "You know perfectly well that Sarah (her older daughter) is allergic to cats."

When they had been living in Riverside Drive they had a long-haired white cat, and nobody had mentioned that it caused a problem. Nobody had said that Sarah had an allergy. Helen reacted as if I had bought the cats out of malice. With her it was always so easy to do the wrong thing. So many times we'd reach a point where I'd breathe a sigh of relief and think "At last, we've sorted ourselves out, and everything's fine," and each time I'd break some unknown rule and send us back to the drawing board.

I called around one day just before lunch, and she asked me if I'd like something to eat. It was the first time I'd ever been offered anything. "I'd love to," I replied.

"I could make an omelette," she said, and then, "Oh, no, I forgot, you don't like my omelettes."

It had been nearly 15 years since the omelette episode that had led to me running away from home. I went out and bought us fish and chips.

Tony's mother arrived for a 6-week visit, and I was determined to make her as welcome as I possibly could and swallow any aggravation. It was a battle lost before it had begun. Within a couple of hours of arrival she had pronounced the house too small. Tony should not be getting his hands dirty working on engines. A foreman wore a white coat and carried a pencil and clipboard, supervising other people. The children were not dressed properly and they shouldn't be left to play outside the house unsupervised.

My hands, which had always flared up under stress, became swollen and inflamed and intolerably itchy. Working with fabric all day further irritated them. I could cook, push a vacuum cleaner around and load and unload the washing machine, but washing dishes was impossible. Any water on my hands was agony, and they were too swollen and painful to feed into rubber gloves. Mamma was outraged that I expected Tony to wash up after a hard day at work. But she didn't offer to do so herself. I heard her telling him I needed a good beating. I ran around to my neighbours and phoned the police, to ask if they would send an officer to the house to have a word with Tony.

"Don't worry, my love," chuckled the police person on the end of the line. "It probably won't happen. Just sounds like a bit of domestic disagreement. We don't get involved in that sort of thing."

"Why don't you?"

"Well, if we intervene the next thing you know, husband and wife are back in each others' arms, and we've wasted our time."

"I can assure you that in this case that's not going to happen."

"If he hasn't hit you we can't do anything. But if he does, give us a call and then we'll come."

"If he does," I said flatly, "I won't be in any condition to call you."

"Cheer up, love!" said the police person.

I put the phone down, stamped back to the house and told Tony and his mother that I'd reported them both to the police for threatening behaviour.

Nothing could please Mamma. Her little rosebud mouth was permanently pursed in disapproval. Her visit lasted almost two weeks, until the day we took her out to Windsor. After a stroll around the town we went to an Italian restaurant for lunch, for which I'd be paying. I'd chosen artichokes for a starter, but the waiter brought sardines. Very politely I reminded him that it was artichokes, and not sardines that I had ordered. He apologised, but at the same time Tony raised his eyes to the ceiling, and with a wave of his arm cried

*"Sempre si lamenta!"* – which translates as "She's always complaining."

*"Ah si, si,"* nodded Mama in agreement.

I picked up the car keys from the table, walked out of the restaurant, climbed into the car, and drove back to St Albans, leaving mother and child to find their own way back. After the children had come home from school and gone to bed that evening, I chopped up the dressing gown Mamma had given me, and half a dozen pairs of my sister-in-law's second-hand tights sent to me as a gift, dumped them in the sink and went to bed. I heard Tony and his mother come back very late at night.

The next day Mamma left. Watching her straight little back marching towards the car with Tony carrying her case, I hated myself.

When Tony returned – if he did – we could not go on living like this. There was no point. None of us was happy. I'd suffered from my parents' divorce, and my children would also suffer. But would they suffer more being brought up in a household with a drunken father who showed no interest in them, and a mother who was struggling to hold herself together?

I'd never asked my father for anything. The previous winter he had bought me a warm coat because I couldn't afford one and he had seen the flimsy jacket I wore. He'd also seen for himself that Tony spent almost no time with the children, he knew he spent all his wages on himself and that I had to work to support us, although he felt that I was demeaning myself by working in a factory. I went to ask for his moral support, and said I was going to start divorce proceedings.

His face clouded over.

"Look, Sue. Divorce isn't a good idea. It's a nasty business, and it would upset Helen. You know how she feels. It reminds her of, well, of the past. Now why don't you go home, have a bottle of wine and make up your quarrel, whatever it's about. You know that Tony thinks the world of you."

Well, the last thing I wanted to do was upset Helen by reminding her that my father had divorced my mother nearly 20 years previously.

I went home. It was my eighth wedding anniversary, so I stopped at the supermarket and bought a bottle of pink Lambrusco, some smoked salmon and some chocolate mousse. I had no idea where Tony was.

When Rob and Julie came home from school I told them that their grandmother had had to go home suddenly. I fed and bathed them and we sat together watching television until their bedtime.

Then I sat in my bedroom, looking at myself in the dressing table mirror for a long time. What was wrong with me? Why couldn't I get along with Mamma and Helen? Did I really deserve all this grief? I thought about what I'd done. I'd married somebody so that I could keep my horse. I'd been selfish and thoughtless and I'd spoiled Tony's life and that of his parents. My father was disappointed and ashamed of me because I worked in a factory. The longer I looked at myself the more guilty and worthless I felt. I was a failure as a daughter, as a mother and as a wife. Yes, I'd earned the grief.

I had a bath and washed my hair, and made myself up. I wrote a note to my father apologising for all I had done wrong, asking forgiveness, and leaving instructions about my children's future. Then I took a crystal glass from the shelf. I prepared a salad with the smoked salmon, and opened the bottle of Lambrusco. I sat at the table, eating the salad and sipping the wine. Beside me was a bottle of the anti-histamines I took for hay fever, a bottle of strong painkillers prescribed for back pain, and one of Valium the doctor had prescribed because I couldn't sleep. I ate the salad and chocolate mousse, sipping the wine and swallowing a few pills with every mouthful. When the last spoonful of mousse was gone, I tucked myself into bed with the bottle and the glass and the remaining tablets, and sipped the wine and swallowed tablets, weeping with self-pity, until I was tired enough to sleep.

I was being carried down the stairs and out into the night.

"Open your eyes, my darling, show me your beautiful eyes."

I stared into a kindly face, and wanted to ask who he was, but I couldn't speak.

"Come on darling, keep them open. Let me see those lovely eyes.

196

My, they're so green! Keep them open; keep looking at me, that's my good girl. Look at me."

It was so wonderful to hear a caring voice. I tried to keep looking into the eyes that the voice was coming out of, but I was so very tired and there seemed to be two faces.

We were moving fast, and each time I forced my beautiful green eyes open for the gentle voice, I saw a blue flash through the window.

The vehicle stopped and I was being wheeled through the night air, so terribly weary and I just couldn't keep opening my eyes any more, even for the kind voice. I didn't want to.

My stomach contents splashed noisily into a galvanised bucket via a thick tube going down my throat, and that was the last thing I remembered.

Two days later I opened my eyes to see Tony sitting beside me, pinch-faced and overflowing with indignation.

"How could you do such a thing?" he shouted. "What are the neighbours going to think of me?"

Really, you have to laugh.

My father and Helen visited, and said soothing things and reminded me how Tony thought the world of me.

Failed suicide patients received no sympathy. An ill-tempered nurse slapped my meals on a table – sometimes she put her head around the curtains surrounding my bed (I was in disgrace and kept screened off from the other patients, who were genuinely ill), and snapped "Your food's on the table." Sometimes she didn't, and it was up to me to guess, collect it and retire to the curtained cell.

After a week I was discharged from the hospital, and given an appointment to see a psychiatrist. When I met him I realised he was quite insane.

"How are you feeling?" he asked.

"I'm fine, thank you."

"What does 'fine' mean?"

"It means I'm OK."

"What do you mean by 'OK'?"

I said "For Christ sake! What do you want me to say?"

197

We talked for ten minutes about the reason I had tried to kill myself. Then he said it sounded as if it was not me, but Tony he should be talking to, and he didn't need to see me again.

When I mentioned it, Tony replied: "I'm not seeing a psychiatrist, you're the one who's mad," and that was the end of the discussion.

# Chapter Twenty-nine

## Endgame

I went to see a solicitor, and asked him to write to Tony saying that I was going to divorce him. The letter arrived on a Saturday morning. Tony lay on the floor and wrapped his arms around my ankles, swearing he would change, he'd stop drinking, contribute to the upkeep of the family and house. He wept and beat his head on the floor and begged me to give him one more chance. Out of pity, I agreed. His good intentions lasted until the Monday. My solicitor drew up divorce proceedings.

Living under the same roof as Tony was more than a nightmare, it simply became intolerable. I had put the children together in one bedroom, and moved into a separate room. I regularly woke as the front door smashed open in the early hours of the morning, further demolishing the cardboard dividing wall. Tony bounced off the walls, tripped up the stairs, staggered into the bathroom to vomit. Once he came into my room and stood panting and growling beside the bed. I did my best imitation of being in a deep sleep, whilst simultaneously silently wetting the bed with fear. He had never been physically violent, but his mental state was such that I thought it a possibility, and he was immensely strong. After what felt like a very long time he stamped from the room, banging the door behind him while I lay experiencing the familiar wet sensation I had felt in Orange dormitory at boarding school all those years ago when I'd unplugged the hot water bottle.

One of us would have to go. I talked with my solicitor and he referred me to a sheltered house for battered wives. I had not been battered, but the fear was always there. Seeing the stained mattresses on the floor, the dishes of half-eaten meals, the dirty nappies and overflowing ash trays, I made my mind up. My children were not going to live in squalor.

I was sympathetic to Tony and tormented with guilt, because it was my selfish actions that had created this horrible situation. I spoke to some friends he had made where he worked and asked if he could stay with them for a while. I didn't discuss the situation with my father and Helen, and they didn't ask. We pretended nothing was wrong.

Now Tony developed a paternal interest in the children. Most evenings he took them out for a meal. I had no wish to stop him seeing them, and as he contributed nothing towards their keep at least if he took them out for a meal it helped financially. When I asked if they'd enjoyed themselves, they said yes, they'd been to see some people and then they'd gone for a meal.

After a few weeks Tony said he was returning to live in Kenya. He was quiet and rational, and we talked for a long time. I apologised, and said that I thought it was for the best, that he would be happier living with his family, and that he could come to see the children whenever he wanted. I would do nothing to try and turn them against him. There was always at the back of my mind the fear that he would try to take the children from the country. Although he had sworn he would never do so, my solicitor had applied to have them made Wards of Court, but the application was denied as the judge didn't feel there was any risk involved. Before the hearing I had to give the children's passports to my solicitor. When he posted them back to me I put them up on a shelf in the sitting room.

One Sunday Tony came to take the children out for the day. He was taking them swimming, and they set off excitedly with their costumes rolled into towels. Since he had moved out, he seemed to have a lot more time for them than he'd ever done before; in fact he had become a doting father. They would be back at 4.00pm, he said. I was in the bathroom when they left, and we all called out to each other, and said "See you later."

At 4.00pm the children were not home. They weren't back by 5.00pm. I phoned the friends where he was living and asked if he was there. No, they said, and put the phone down. When I rang straight back, it was off the hook.

I called my father to say that the children were not back. He and Helen didn't think there was any cause for concern; it was a nice day, they'd probably be back in a while. They told me not to worry.

I phoned the police, and tried to instil in them some of my rising panic. They were fatherly, patronising and not interested. They too told me not to worry, my husband would be back later with my little ones. I already knew, in my heart and stomach, that he would not. Could they just, I pleaded, go to where Tony had been living and see if he was there? (When Tony left, the car had gone with him. I had bought a bicycle for getting back and forwards to work.) I persuaded them that a ten-minute drive couldn't do them any harm, and they agreed to go to Tony's lodgings and see if he was there.

They phoned back half an hour later.

"Bad news, I'm afraid, my love. He's gone. All his things have gone. But his friends say they don't know where."

Sick, knowing the worst, I remembered the passports on the shelf. They had gone.

I phoned my solicitor at his home.

The next morning the children were made Wards of Court. An all-ports alert was issued, but we all knew it was already too late.

Because the children had been born in the independent country of Kenya, and because their father was Italian, they were not British subjects and therefore not within the jurisdiction of the British courts. Their father had every right to take them wherever he wished. Further, they could not be taken out of Kenya without his written consent.

My father and Helen didn't seem particularly concerned. Helen kept assuring me that Tony loved me, he was kind, he'd never do anything to hurt me. I should stop worrying, she was sure things would all turn out happily. I wondered how she'd have felt if he'd kidnapped her children.

Nan came to stay with me and without her support I don't know what I would have done.

The next three weeks were a frantic haze of meetings and lengthy telephone conversations with anybody I thought could help: judges, politicians, journalists, diplomats and a private detective. My local MP, Mr Victor Goodhew promised he'd do everything he could. The police said that they were unable to involve Interpol because the children did not appear to be in any danger. I pointed out that Tony was an alcoholic and that his mental state was rather fragile. That wasn't a sufficient threat to the children, they replied.

"What was?" I asked.

They told me what is regarded as a possible danger to children.

"That's what he's been doing," I said.

So Interpol became involved and traced the children to Rome, but from there they disappeared.

Each morning I woke to the fresh reminder that my children had vanished and I'd no idea how, or if, I could get them back. I could not look in their bedrooms and see their empty beds, or their Easter eggs waiting on the shelf, and I couldn't think of anything else except to wonder where and how they were.

One evening I had a phone call from Tony – he wanted me to know the children were safe, they were with him, they were in Kenya, and they weren't coming back. But if I would stop being silly and join them there, we could make a new start. Back with Mamma and the binges, the clinking bottles at midnight, my sister-in-law's old tights and the people who wouldn't risk a refrigerator on me! I didn't think so. I was going to find another way.

I'd spent the 22$^{nd}$ day since Tony had taken the children in London talking to journalists, hoping that somebody would magically find a solution. As I went to catch the train home, a black railway worker stooped and picked up a red rose that had fallen onto the platform, and presented it to me with a little bow. When I got off the train in St Albans there was a rainbow, and walking up the road towards the house, a black cat crossed my path. I was certain that these three incidents were an omen. As I opened the front door the phone was ringing.

A local journalist at that time, Maurice Chittenden, had written about the abduction of the children, and his article had been picked up by a Daily Telegraph journalist named Brenda Parry, who had been crusading for children at risk of being kidnapped and taken out of the country to be made Wards of Court. Wardship was an expensive procedure and difficult to obtain, and the result was that many women lost their children and were powerless to get them back. She had contacted an East African newspaper. They in turn had made enquiries and learned that Tony was in Italy on a training course. He had left the children in Kenya in the care of his sister-in-law. They were phoning me to say that the British Foreign Secretary, David Owen had taken up the matter with the Kenya Government, who were already embarrassed by Tony talking to the press regarding his 'influence over Kenyan politicians.' If I could get on a plane to Kenya next day, the newspaper would guarantee we could get the children back to England.

By this time I had left the factory and managed to find a well-paid secretarial job, and the company I was working for bought me a return ticket to Nairobi. My father and Helen drove me to the airport. At 6.00pm I was one of seven passengers on a Kenyan Airways plane bound for Nairobi.

At the airport next morning a reporter and photographer from the newspaper drove me to my sister-in-law's house. She wasn't there, but the house servant was clearly expecting us. No, she beamed, sincerely, she had absolutely no idea where the children were, but she was very pleased to see me. She would make some coffee. Thank you, we wouldn't be stopping.

We drove to my sister-in-law's office where twitching Venetian blinds indicated we were expected.

The sister-in-law appeared, and asked what all the fuss was about. Why couldn't I just come to visit my children normally, without making all this commotion and talking to the newspapers? The children were ecstatically happy with her. They had their grandparents and cousins, sunshine and a new swing and a slide too. She said the children had never mentioned me. I should be prepared for a shock because they didn't want anything to do with me. But she kept refusing to tell us where they were.

"Madame," said the journalist finally, while the photographer aimed his camera at her, "are you trying to stop this lady from seeing her children?" He scribbled something on his pad.

"Of course not," she snapped.

"Then please tell us where they are."

Through gritted teeth she said they were safely in school, a proper school where they would receive a decent Italian education. They were very happy and didn't want to go back to England. I was making a mistake if I thought they would want to see me.

While she was talking I noticed with satisfaction that since I last saw her, the skin on her neck had developed a texture like crepe paper.

As we drove to the school, I felt sick. What if my children really didn't want to come home with me? Was I taking them away from a better life? Would they be better living in this beautiful country, albeit with an alcoholic father? What would I do if they said they didn't want to come home? If they did, should I respect their wishes and let them stay?

They ran towards me, and I held them in my arms.

"I've come to take you home," I said.

The British High Commission issued the children with temporary British passports. We were taken to a hotel in Nairobi and told to stay in the room, and not to contact anybody. That was hard: I wanted to call friends, but the journalist said that the Italian community in Nairobi were trying to find where we were. It was essential to keep our whereabouts hidden to avoid any problems. There was a surreal James Bond feeling to the situation.

We spent the day in the hotel room. The children told me how their father had promised to take them swimming, but instead had driven them directly to the airport and flown with them to Italy. They had stayed there for a few days with friends, before flying to Kenya. Rob told me that Julie had never stopped asking for me. Both of them seemed to have taken their adventure in their stride.

Rob said: "Don't worry about anything, Mum. I'll get a job and look after us all." He was nine years old.

That evening the journalist drove us back to Nairobi airport. There were no formalities, no immigration, no customs. We swept straight through into the lounge, which to our horror was filled with Italians, all waiting to board the same plane that we were booked on. But they were simply tourists homebound to Rome, who boarded noisily without a glance at us.

Twelve hours after I had arrived in Kenya we were airborne, heading back to England.

At Heathrow Maurice Chittenden was waiting to take us home, where Nan, my father and Helen waited. Helen expressed her sympathy for Tony. He was only trying his best, he didn't mean any harm, he loved me and he loved his children, poor man.

That evening, after the children had gone to bed and after my last guest had left, the phone rang. A distinguished, educated voice that I at first took to be somebody from the Foreign Office, asked whether the children were asleep, and then proceeded to describe in graphic detail exactly what he was going to do to me, bitch from hell that I was, now that all my visitors had left. Somebody was watching my house and knew that I was alone.

"I'll be with you in five minutes," he said.

Insanely, I replied, "Thank you. I'll see you then."

I was very tired. I phoned the local police who were their normal disinterested and unsympathetic selves, and told me not to worry, cranky callers never follow up on their threats. I should just go to bed and forget all about it. Sometimes I wonder what purpose they ever served, apart from telling worried people not to worry, or loitering behind trees trying to catch motorists exceeding the speed limit.

I phoned a casual acquaintance and asked if he would come to the house for the night so that I could sleep.

Later I learned that all those evenings when Tony took the children 'out for a meal' he was building up a support network amongst his friends and people he knew from work. Just popping in to say 'hello' with the children, he would ask them what they had had for supper. They, naturally and truthfully, replied: "Nothing." Of course I hadn't fed them as he said he was taking them out to eat. So with a big sigh Tony would say "Well, I'll take them somewhere to eat – as you can see, their mother doesn't bother to feed them."

205

If any of these people had been intelligent enough they would have seen that the children were well-dressed, clean, healthy and well-fed. But I don't think they wanted to see that, I think they were enjoying being part of a drama.

That's how Tony convinced a group of people who should have known better to help him kidnap the children. That's how he instilled in these people such hatred that they made anonymous phone calls threatening me with things so vile I can't write them. I couldn't help but be impressed by his cunning.

He came back to England to fight for custody. While we waited outside the courtroom, I asked him why and said that he wouldn't win, but that I would let him see the children whenever he wanted to. He replied that he knew he couldn't win, but that his family insisted he tried. Even at 40 he was still a child acting on Mamma's orders.

My father supported my application for custody by writing a statement to the effect that Tony had played no noticeable part in the children's upbringing or entertainment.

The presiding judge was Justice James Kingham, a kind and very family-orientated man who made the proceedings as relaxed as possible. He said he would like to have a little chat privately with Rob. I went and collected him from school and explained on the way to court that a very nice man wanted to talk to him. "You be honest, and answer his questions. Whatever you say, nobody will be angry or upset with you. All you need to do is to tell the truth, tell him how you feel."

History was almost repeating itself. A child was being asked to choose between his parents.

When Rob and Justice Kingham emerged from their chat, the judge said: "After speaking to Rob, I find that he is a very English little boy, and I am therefore going to give custody to his mother. But he is to retain his Italian surname, and his father should be allowed access to him in England."

# Chapter Thirty

## Final Curtain

A year after he lost the custody case, Tony came to England planning to spend two weeks visiting the children.

Surprisingly, my father and Helen suggested that Rob and Julie should stay with them. They would hold Tony's passport, and he could collect the children from them daily and return them each evening. It was the most support they had ever offered. They emphasised that they would not discuss with Tony any of the events that had taken place, any more than they wanted to know my side of the story. They perched determinedly on the fence.

"We do not want to be involved, or take sides," my father explained bluntly.

For the first two days of his visit I phoned in the evenings to ask if everything was alright. Yes, said my father, the children were fine and Tony was behaving.

On the third day Helen telephoned me at work.

"Come and collect your children," she said. "Take them away, and don't ever bring them back."

We went to collect them, and found them standing anxiously in the hallway of my father's house, dressed in their hats and coats, packed bags beside them, all the doors leading into the house firmly closed. My father, Helen and their two daughters stood in a defensive row like rugby fullbacks, as if blocking off attempts by us to force our way into their house.

They pushed the children forward, and told us never to come back. No reason or explanation was offered.

I didn't ask for one – as you might remember, our unspoken rule was "Don't speak."

I said nothing, just took the children and their cases and put them in the car and drove away.

Tony had returned to Kenya.

About 18 months later I received a note from my father. It was the first communication I'd had since our exile. I had sent Christmas and birthday cards to all the family except Helen, but there had been nothing from them, not for me and not for the children. It seemed as if we had ceased to exist, and yet I felt certain in the back of my mind that eventually my father and I would meet again. When I saw the envelope with his perfect handwriting on it I felt a great wave of relief and pleasure, knowing that he was offering an opportunity for us to put the past behind us. We'd meet for a drink somewhere and talk things over. It would be a little awkward at first, I expected. He'd explain what had gone wrong between us. I'd apologise for whatever it was, and then he'd tell one of his mildly risky jokes. We'd have a laugh, a hug, and move on from there.

His letter was short. It said:

*'Dear Sue*
*You still have my slide carousel"* (which we'd borrowed to look at some transparencies)*, "and I have a number of Premium Bonds I bought for the children. We should sort these out – the Bonds should be put in the children's names as I'm not getting any younger. Perhaps we could meet on neutral ground.*
*Bob'*

I stared in disbelief at the words 'neutral ground'. What the hell did that mean? Why were we at war? And who was Bob? Where had Daddy gone?

This was not the hand of peace; it was the final stage of divorce, tying up the last few loose ends so that we need never meet again. If I replied, it would be over forever. I couldn't face that. If I ignored the letter, in time there would be another approach where we could make our peace.

I asked a friend to return the carousel, and tore up the letter. And heard no more.

Three years later, Tony contacted my solicitor and asked to see the children. We arranged to meet in a local restaurant. Enough time had passed for us to be able to at least be civil to each other.

We sat politely drinking beer and asking how this person was, and how that person was. He had brought me a couple of photographs of Cinderella in her old age, standing in the sunshine against the backdrop of the Ngong Hills.

Then he suddenly said how sorry he was to hear about my father. What about him, I asked?

"But you must know," he said.

"Know what?"

He handed me a letter in Helen's handwriting. The envelope was addressed to the Italian Consulate in Nairobi, dated a year previously. It asked them to forward it to Tony. In it she wrote to tell him that my father had died, after a year's illness.

As I read the letter it felt as if my heart would burst.

"You didn't know," Tony said. "Nobody told you?"

"No," I replied. "They didn't tell me."

He looked stunned, disbelieving. "I always liked your father very much. He was a nice man," he said.

I could hardly think. My mind seemed to have closed down.

Mechanically we arranged that he would collect the children from our house the following day.

He came for them in the morning, and returned them a few hours later. Without explanation he returned to Kenya the next day.

I rang Aunt Veronica. Since the breakdown of my relationship with my father I hadn't had any contact with her either. I felt very bitter towards the whole family.

"Is this true, what I've been told? That my father is dead?"

"Yes. He had leukaemia," she replied.

"Why did nobody tell me?" I asked.

"I thought you should be told, but neither he nor Helen wanted it."

"Where is he buried?" I asked.

"He isn't. He died in St Thomas' Hospital in London. Helen had him cremated and his ashes scattered. There is nothing left of him."

My father had been dead for a year, and dying for a year before that. Helen had gone to the trouble of contacting Tony, but not telling me. And there wasn't even a memorial to him.

I still find it incomprehensible that anybody could be quite so callous.

I made a list of everything I knew about my father.

He was tall, thin, blonde and blue-eyed.

At school he'd played cricket.

He'd boxed for his school – Battersea Grammar.

He'd been in the war.

He'd ridden a motorbike.

He'd suffered from migraines.

He'd smoked a pipe.

He'd once had a moustache.

He'd been an accountant.

He'd liked dogs.

His fair skin sunburned easily.

Pansies were his favourite flowers.

He'd liked telling slightly risqué jokes.

He seldom drank apart from an occasional beer.

When he was a schoolboy, he and his friends had amused themselves by tying people's door-knockers together and then running away. They also used to stuff paper up inside telephone boxes where money was returned if a call was not collected, so that people often gave up pressing button B to get their money back. The little boys went round in the evenings removing the paper and any unclaimed money.

When I was a little girl, he would tear off and give me the pictures of swans from inside of boxes of Swan Vesta matches.

He'd been married twice, divorced once, and had had four children.

The last time I could remember him hugging me was before I left to go to boarding school.

I had never danced with him.

That's all I know. It isn't very much.

210

Tony never saw the children again. Neither he nor his family maintained any contact with them until ten years later, when he sent them two fairly large sums of money, and said he would be coming to England to visit them. But he never arrived. He subsequently died of alcohol-related illness.

I married the man who came to the house on the night I returned with the children from Kenya, and we have been together ever since. He willingly and whole-heartedly took on the role of father to Rob and Julie, paying for their education, their food, clothes, toys, holidays and treats, helping them, loving them, and supporting them in all their highs and lows.

For many years two things haunted me. I kept hearing the words of hate Helen had spat out on the day I'd walked out of the house in Riverside Drive.

"And it's about time somebody told you the truth about your...", and I kept seeing the signature on the bottom of my father's note – 'Bob'.

I phoned Auntie Veronica. We didn't have any contact apart from exchanging cards at Christmas, but she was the only person still alive who could answer my question.

"Was he my real father?" I asked.

"Of course he was," she replied. "Why on earth would you ask such a question?"

"Because of something Helen once said. And because the last time he wrote to me he signed his name as Bob. And because even when he knew he was dying he didn't contact me."

"Well, he certainly was your father," she repeated, "and he worried about you a great deal."

Well, I suppose that was better than nothing.

Had he wished I'd chosen differently all those years ago when he told me to choose between him and Mummy? Had he wished I'd left with her and not complicated his life? I'm fairly sure he had. I think I lost him from the day I went into hospital in Nairobi, when he met Helen.

Aunt Veronica phoned again some time later.

"Helen's dying. She's asked for your address as she wants to write to you. I said I'd ask you."

I thought back to that unfinished sentence and wondered if I really wanted to know the rest. Would she write something to raise me up, or knock me further down? It was a risk I couldn't take.

"Don't give her my address. I don't want to hear from her."

After her death, one of my half-sisters contacted me. She gave me a pearl tie-pin that I had once given my father for his birthday. It is all I have of him.

# Epilogue

For many, many years after I heard of his death, I did not know how I felt about my father. I knew I was hurt and angry, and I knew that I wished with all my heart that he had never married Helen, as I wished equally that I had replied to his last letter to me when there was still time.

Aunt Veronica once said that he was a weak man, who gave in rather than fight, and I think that was probably true. He was gentle, and honest, and correct, and handsome, and never showed the least sign of aggression. But I felt he had let me down after he married Helen. He had taken the easy road of placating her to my cost.

Whenever I did think of him, I remembered him sobbing after Mummy left, when he told me I was going to boarding school. That was the only time I had ever seen any real emotion in him.

Over and over I asked myself why, when he knew he was dying, hadn't he contacted me? Had he so totally rejected me and my children that we had stopped existing for him? Was he too ill to be bothered? I did not want his money – I learned from a close family friend that he had made provision for the children in his will, but it never materialised – but could he not have at least left a letter, just a few words? Or did he want to save me from the pain of witnessing his illness and death? I'll never know, just as I'll never know why we were so dramatically and thoroughly banished from his world.

Twenty years passed before I found an answer to my question, which was how I felt about him.

I dreamed, one night. I was walking down a busy road, and ahead of me, crossing through the traffic, was a familiar slender figure in a familiar beige gaberdine raincoat, walking very slowly, with his head slightly bowed. At the moment when I realised it was my father, I saw him stumble and fall. Whether he had been hit by a car, or tripped, or had a heart attack, I don't know, but I saw him falling and ran to try and catch him. It was too late. He lay motionless on the pavement. Then he was lying in a hospital bed, with the blankets and sheet pulled up under his chin, and his arms resting on the covers and his eyes closed. I was sitting beside him, holding and stroking his hand. He opened his eyes and looked into my face, and I said: "It's OK, Daddy, you're going to be fine. You're going to be just fine. I'm here with you." He smiled weakly, and squeezed my hand.

I woke up, and my pillow and face were wet, and I knew that I had loved him.

Looking back I remember all the kind people who owed me nothing but gave me so much. All those people who in one way or another made life easier when it was hard, and happier when it was sad. I thank them all.

This has been so hard to write. I've felt myself drowning in a sea of tears and nostalgia as I remembered the days at Machakos, and my time with Cinderella and yearned to return to them. In some ways they were the worst of times, but in many other ways they were the very best.

As I've been writing, I've tried to see events through the eyes of the other people involved. Did they interpret my solitude and self-sufficiency as sullenness? Did they just see a selfish girl, or one who was trying to survive the only way she could? I don't like what I think they saw. With the benefit of hindsight, I think we could have all tried harder and done a little better. But at the time, we were doing the best we could.

Still, there are some people to whom I feel I should apologise.

To Nan, who I took for granted and never appreciated as much as she deserved, never considering how hard her life had been, losing a child and a grandchild, and never thanking her enough for her support and loyalty. Before we left to live in Kenya, I gave her a thruppenny piece. Thirty years later, when she died, I found it amongst her few belongings. She had had a link fixed to it, so that she could wear it on her bracelet.

To Tony and Mamma, for obvious reasons.

To Daddy for not replying to his note.

And to Mummy, for not screaming and shouting and protesting that day in the living room on Lower Kabete Road. For betraying her by just letting her walk away.

I wish they were all still here so that I could say "I'm sorry."

# Photographs

This photo was given to me by my second cousin, Betty. It is the
only photograph I have of my mother and father together. It is
unusual in that Granny, Granddad and Nan are all together and
smiling. I am sitting on Nan's knee, front right. My mother and
father are behind. Granny and Granddad are holding my cousins on
their knees, and my aunts and uncles stand behind them.

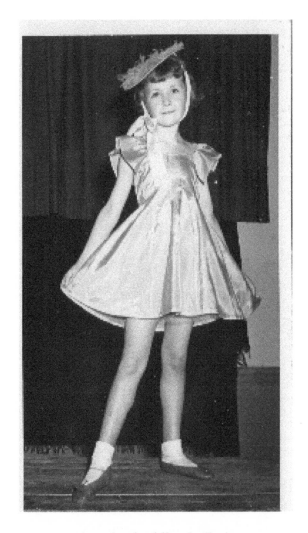

Age 6, a budding ballerina

Outside the house in Lower Kabete Road, Nairobi. 1954

Ready for a ride on Wimbledon Common, 1957

The happiest 14-year-old girl, with Cinderella

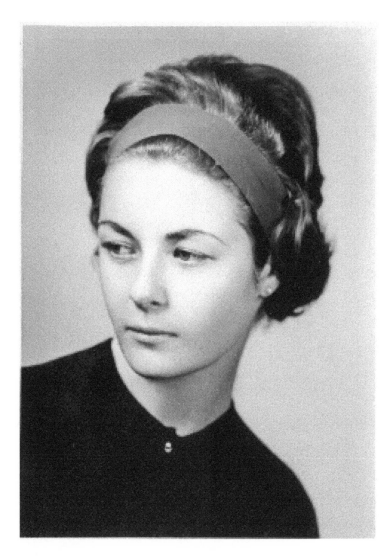

At 18

Me with Cindy and my two little half-sisters. Helen, who was
standing to the right, cut herself out of the photo.

My friend Vivien riding Cinderella

Wedding day

My little brother Ian, shortly before his death

Mummy, taken in about 1938

Mummy with my step-father John, and their little girl

This is the only other photograph I have of my father. I am
standing on the right, holding Julie. On my fathers right is one of my
half-sisters. Rob is standing in the foreground. 1971

My lovely house servant, Mwiba, with Rob

With Nan, on holiday in Boscombe, 1949

Cinderella in retirement at the foot of the Ngong Hills

[1] http://lwmcferrin.com/
[2] Sir
[3] Mistress
[4] Little mistress
[5] He/she doesn't understand Swahili
[6] A sort of thatch made from coco palm leaves
[7] you
[8] come here
[9] "the boss"
[10] food
[11] chicken
[12] oven
[13] not me
[14] Kikuyu greeting
[15] Yes, mistress

# Acknowledgements

With very many thanks to Andrew Ives for his meticulous proof-reading, and loan of eight packets of commas.

Also to Linda Watanabe McFerrin (http://www.lwmcferrin.com/), intrepid traveller, prolific author and writing teacher, for her kind permission to quote her beautifully-written passage about the Lunatic Line.

# About The Author

Born a Londoner, Susie Kelly spent most of the first 25 years of her life in Kenya. She now lives in south-west France with her husband and assorted animals. She's slightly scatterbrained and believes that compassion, courage and a sense of humour are the three essentials for surviving life in the 21st century. She gets on best with animals, eccentrics, and elderly people.

CONNECT WITH SUSIE KELLY
http://about.me/susie.kelly

# More Susie Kelly Books

*Best Foot Forward – A 500-Mile Walk Through Hidden France* (Transworld 2000/Blackbird 2011) A touching and inspiring tale of the Texan pioneering spirit, English eccentricity, and two women old enough to know better. (Also available as an audiobook on Amazon Audible and iTunes)

*The Valley of Heaven and Hell – Cycling in the Shadow of Marie-Antoinette* (Blackbird 2011) Novice cyclist Susie bikes 500 miles through Paris and Versailles, the battlefields of World War 1, the Champagne region and more

*Two Steps Backward* (Bantam 2004) The trials and tribulations of moving a family and many animals from the UK to a run-down smallholding in SW France.

*Travels With Tinkerbelle, 6,000 Miles Around France In A Mechanical Wreck* (Blackbird 2012) The author and her husband devised a simple plan – to take a tent and the dog and drive around the perimeter of France. Like many simple plans it went wrong before it started.

*Swallow & Robins – The Guests In My Garden* (Blackbird 2012) The true story of a beginner's attempts at running two holiday homes in remotest France and her love/hate relationship with her guests. (Blackbird 2013)

# More Blackbird Digital Books

*The Dream Theatre* by Sarah Ball (2011)
*That Special Someone* (2014) by Tanya Bullock
*A London Steal – The Fabulous-On-A-Budget Guide to London's Hidden Chic* by Elle Ford (2013)
*Cats Through History* by Christina Hamilton (2012)
*The Modigliani Girl* by Jacqui Lofthouse (2015)
*Schizophrenia – Who Cares? – A Father's Story* (2013) by Tim Salmon
*The Widow's To Do List* by Stephanie Zia (2011)

238

If you've enjoyed this book please would you consider leaving a review on Amazon USA or Amazon UK? A couple of lines is plenty. It really makes all the difference to us small independent publishers who rely on word of mouth to get our books known. Thank you!

Keep up to date with Susie Kelly news and new books by joining
the Susie Kelly mailing list.
Email your contact details to
blackbird-digibooks@gmail.com
(Managed securely by Mailchimp, details are never, ever shared
with any third parties)

**Blackbird Digital Books**
**London**
http://blackbird-books.com/
blackbird.digibooks@gmail.com

239

Lightning Source UK Ltd.
Milton Keynes UK
UKHW040156180221
378934UK00002B/363